THE
LSU
RURAL LIFE MUSEUM
& Windrush Gardens

THE

LSU

RURAL LIFE MUSEUM

& Windrush Gardens

A LIVING HISTORY

FAYE PHILLIPS

THE
History
PRESS

Published by The History Press
Charleston, SC 29403
www.historypress.net

Cover images: Front, top image courtesy of Darelyn Marshall, the LSU Rural Life Museum
and Windrush Gardens; front, bottom image courtesy of Jim Zietz, LSU University
Relations; back, left image courtesy of Nancy N. Colyar; back, right image courtesy of the
LSU Rural Life Museum.

First published 2010

ISBN 9781540234551

Phillips, Faye.
The LSU Rural Life Museum and Windrush Gardens : a living history / Faye Phillips.
p. cm.
Includes bibliographical references and index.

1. LSU Rural Life Museum (Baton Rouge, La.) 2. Windrush Gardens (Baton Rouge, La.)
3. Country life--Louisiana--History. 4. Plantation life--Louisiana--History. 5. Material
culture--Louisiana--History. 6. Vernacular architecture--Louisiana--History. 7. Louisiana-
-Social life and customs. 8. Mississippi River Valley--Social life and customs. 9. Burden
family. 10. Baton Rouge (La.)--Biography. I. Title.
F370.P47 2010
307.72074'76318--dc22
2010016297

Notice: The information in this book is true and complete to the best of our knowledge. It is
offered without guarantee on the part of the author or The History Press. The author and
The History Press disclaim all liability in connection with the use of this book.

I dedicate this book to Ione and Steele Burden and to the Burden and related families.

CONTENTS

Contents

ACKNOWLEDGEMENTS

I gratefully acknowledge the assistance of the staff of the Louisiana State University (LSU) Libraries Special Collections and the staff of the LSU Rural Life Museum and Windrush Gardens. Without their help this book could not have been completed. In particular, Judy Bolton and Gabe Harrell solved reference and scanning problems. The majority of the images in the book are from the LSU Rural Life Museum Collections, the LSU Libraries Special Collections, the Louisiana and Lower Mississippi Valley Collections and the University Archives. A special thanks to photographers Jim Zietz of LSU University Relations and Nancy N. Colyar of the LSU Libraries for sharing their wonderful color images of the Windrush Gardens.

Finally, many thanks to friends and colleagues who read drafts of the text and aided with their excellent editorial eyes: Elaine Smyth, Jennifer Cargill, David Floyd and Nancy Colyar. Family and friends were patient, polite and supportive as they listened again and again to the great stories about the Rural Life Museum and Windrush Gardens.

Caption Credit Abbreviations:

The Ione Burden and Family Papers, MSS 3063, Louisiana and Lower Mississippi Valley Collections, LSU Libraries, Baton Rouge, Louisiana. Cited as the Burden Family Papers, LLMVC, LSU Libraries.

The LSU Photograph Collection, Office of Public Relations Records, RG A5000.0020, University Archives, LSU Libraries, Baton Rouge, Louisiana.

ACKNOWLEDGEMENTS

Cited as the LSU Photograph Collection, Office of Public Relations, UA, LSU Libraries.

The LSU Photograph Collection, School of Architecture Records, RG A5000.0901, University Archives, LSU Libraries, Baton Rouge, Louisiana. Cited as the LSU Photograph Collection, School of Architecture, UA, LSU Libraries.

INTRODUCTION

L eave the noise of busy streets, a hectic cityscape and sirens from emergency vehicles rushing to nearby hospitals as you turn onto a quiet blacktop lane edged by a multitude of seasonal blooming plants. Follow the lane past true farmland still existing in the twenty-first century. Continue as it curves around a field of rose plants, across a narrow bridge and around more curves. Slow down until you see an oak *allée* and granite columns that once graced a library entrance. You, your family and any pet mules, oxen and chickens are always welcome. You have just entered the grounds of the Louisiana State University's Rural Life Museum and Windrush Gardens. Welcome back to the life lived in rural nineteenth-century Louisiana.

Burden family members Ione, Steele, Pike and Pike's wife, Jeanette, made the decision in 1966 to donate their family plantation, Windrush, to Louisiana State University (LSU). Ione, Pike and Steele, the last direct Burden descendants, were the children of William Stephen Pike Burden Sr. and Ollie Brice Steele Burden, who acquired Windrush Plantation from his great-uncle's heirs. This remarkable act of generosity resulted in a permanent green space in the center of Baton Rouge. At the time, it was the largest gift ever received by LSU, at an estimated value of $270 million (in 1966 currency). The Burden Foundation was incorporated by the Burdens in October 1961 as a nonprofit organization focused on "benevolent, charitable, educational and religious purposes." Its role regarding Windrush Plantation was to administer the donation and oversee compliance with the requirements of the gift.[1]

Five acres were dedicated to the LSU Rural Life Museum, the dream of Steele Burden, who developed it with the help and support of his sister

The LSU Rural Life Museum and Windrush Gardens are a permanent green space in the heart of Baton Rouge, Louisiana. *Courtesy of Darelyn Marshall, the LSU Rural Life Museum and Windrush Gardens.*

Ione, LSU chancellor emeritus Cecil G. Taylor and LSU Agricultural Center chancellor J. Norman Efferson. In 1970, the museum began with a small collection of eighteenth- and nineteenth-century artifacts collected by various LSU faculty and students. Steele Burden added his own collections to LSU's own. Today those two small artifact collections have grown to fill a large exhibit hall, thirty-five buildings (themselves artifacts of the museum) and various exterior exhibits, along with the Windrush Gardens.[2] This book presents the history and remarkable story of the LSU Rural Life Museum and Windrush Gardens.

"The Rural Life Museum's mission is to provide and sustain a publicly accessible center for the collection, preservation, and interpretation of the material culture, cultural landscapes and vernacular architecture of Louisiana and the Lower Mississippi River Valley." Through interpretation and preservation of the collections and buildings, the museum seeks to increase appreciation of the way of life of eighteenth- and nineteenth-century Louisianans, their hardships, toils, vision, determination and inspiration. The Rural Life Museum holds the largest collection of Louisiana vernacular (folk) architecture and the most extensive collection of material

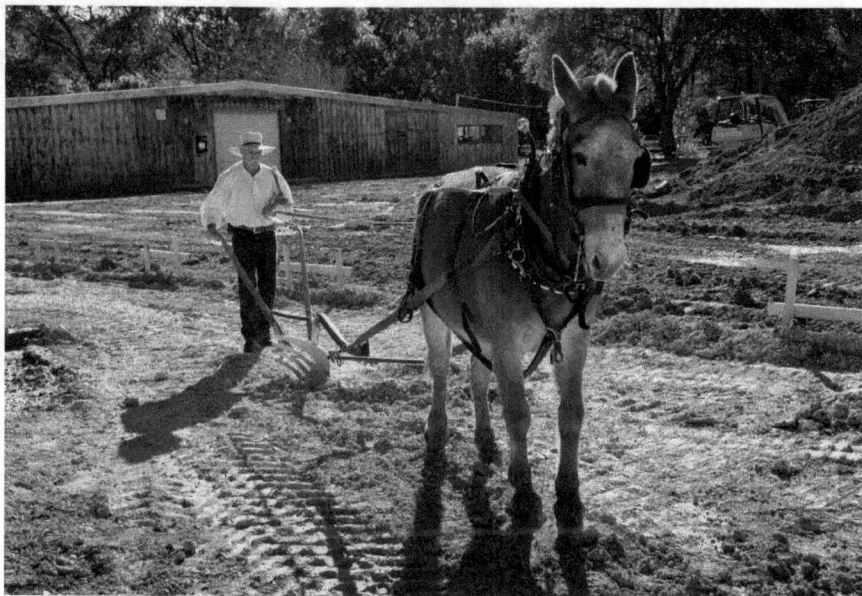

Reminiscent of Louisiana's nineteenth-century rural life, Bill (right) and Melvin plow land at the Rural Life Museum. *Courtesy of Jim Zietz, LSU University Relations.*

culture artifacts from the eighteenth and nineteenth centuries and shows how settlers of Louisiana established an admirable society in spite of great odds. In its forty years of service, the annual visitor count to the museum has increased to over sixty thousand. Its operating budget is over 80 percent self-generated.[3]

More than one hundred volunteer adult docents and over fifty-five junior docents from the sixth through the twelfth grades provide an average of 11,500 hours of service per year. The museum's educational programs aid in the teaching of Louisiana's required K–12 lesson plans, and it serves as a classroom and laboratory for LSU, the Baton Rouge Community College and scholars free of charge. Other visitors include organized tour groups from throughout the world, historical interest groups, church groups, tourists interested in the "Louisiana" experience and local citizens seeking the quiet of Baton Rouge's green space. The British Museum lists the Rural Life Museum as one of the "Top 10 Outdoor Museums in the World," and it has been the conference host for national and international museum associations, as well as the site for hundreds of other cultural agency meetings and programs.[4]

Oxen Buck and Bull often visit the Rural Life Museum. *Courtesy of the LSU Rural Life Museum and Windrush Gardens.*

On the twenty-fifth anniversary of the LSU Rural Life Museum, 1995, the official name was changed to the LSU Rural Life Museum and Windrush Gardens. Ollie Brice Steele Burden and her youngest son, Steele, established the Windrush Gardens in 1921. They landscaped the grounds around the original circa 1856 Windrush House, first using ideas and art objects, especially statuary, that Steele had collected on trips to Europe, Latin America and South America. Ten acres were eventually transformed into beautiful gardens using plants and trees that thrive in Louisiana's harsh weather. Miss Ollie, Steele and Ione all loved and tended to the gardens. About 1926, the family allowed the LSU Agricultural Center faculty to begin agricultural research activities on the Burden property.[5]

William Pike Burden Sr. acquired Windrush Plantation in 1905 and began to raise cattle there. Miss Ollie, a widow after 1925, learned to raise cattle and leased land to tenant farmers. Ione in 1917 worked for LSU and then moved away to work at Louisiana Tech in Ruston, Louisiana. She then moved on to the College of William and Mary in Williamsburg, Virginia, returning permanently to Baton Rouge to live at Windrush and work at LSU

Windrush Plantation as viewed from the air. *Courtesy of the LSU Rural Life Museum and Windrush Gardens.*

in 1933. Pike developed a prosperous printing business in Baton Rouge and always lived there. Steele worked for Baton Rouge City Parks Department and then at LSU as a landscaper, and he lived in Baton Rouge and New Orleans and traveled worldwide. About 1934, Miss Ollie divided twenty-two acres among the three children: Ione received the Windrush House and the land around it, with the gardens that became part of the Rural Life Museum and Windrush Gardens; Pike and wife Jeanette Monroe Burden received land for a new home they built near the original house that continues to remain in the Monroe family; and Steele's tract was heavily wooded land, which also became part of the Rural Life Museum and Windrush Gardens.[6]

Starting in 1966, the Burdens gave 50 acres at a time to the university until 440 acres were donated. LSU was restricted, by the act of donation, in the ways it could use Windrush Plantation, and any violation of the conditions would result in the property reverting to the Burden Foundation. It was to be used only for academic buildings and complexes; gardens;

Above: Plantation bells called everyone to work, meals and the beginning and end of each day. *Courtesy of the LSU Rural Life Museum and Windrush Gardens.*

Left: Steele's sketch shows Pike's house at Windrush Plantation. *Courtesy of the Burden Family Papers, LLMVC, LSU Libraries.*

experimental purposes relating to agriculture; parks or arboretums; forest and wildlife reserves; and caretakers' residences—to be administered by the LSU Agricultural Center. It was also stipulated that the wooded portions of Windrush were to remain as natural wilderness areas.[7] The final 50 acres of Windrush Plantation were donated in 1992. In 1970, Steele Burden moved six historical buildings to Windrush Plantation, which initiated the establishment of the Rural Life Museum complex, and a large barn was constructed to house Steele's collection of nineteenth-century Louisiana artifacts.

The LSU Agricultural Center continued agricultural research on the Burden Research Center (Windrush Plantation), as well as maintained several important named areas and gardens: the Windrush Natural Area and trails (based on a Steele Burden design); the Violet Stone Camellia Garden (moved to the Burden Center in 2002); the All-American Rose Garden (renovated and made a member of the national All-American Rose Selections in 2005); and the International Hibiscus Garden (begun in 2008). Ione died in 1983, and the LSU Agricultural Center named a meeting

Visitors are greeted by busts of Ione and Steele Burden at a new exhibit center opened in 2010. *Courtesy of the LSU Rural Life Museum and Windrush Gardens.*

You are always welcome. The Rural Life Museum and Windrush Gardens are open 360 days per year. *Courtesy of the LSU Rural Life Museum and Windrush Gardens.*

facility and office building (the Ione E. Burden Conference Center) in her honor. Also important is the Steele Burden Memorial Orangerie, developed and donated after Steele's death in 1995.

In 2010, a new Visitors' and Exhibit Center opened for the celebration of the Rural Life Museum's fortieth anniversary, a culmination of the successful Whispers of Change campaign for the future development and improvement of the LSU Rural Life Museum and Windrush Gardens. At the entrance on either side of a vintage wooden wall are busts of Steele and Ione Burden. On the wall is written, in his own words, Steele's mission for the Rural Life Museum and Windrush Gardens: "[T]o increase the appreciation of our heritage and the way of life of our ancestors, their hardships, toils, vision, inspiration and determination by preserving something of the architecture and artifacts from our rural past."[8]

Chapter 1

BEGINNINGS

T he people first associated with Windrush Plantation came to colonial
Baton Rouge along with other settlers from England, Germany and
France, as well as many from the United States. The Pikes, Burdens, Barbees,
Steeles, Hugents, Parks and related families arrived as Baton Rouge began
to change from a frontier outpost to a busy river port and then, in 1846,
to Louisiana's state capital. These families became important citizens and
community leaders in Baton Rouge.[9]

William Stephen Pike (1820–1875), originally from Kentucky, was in Baton
Rouge by 1850, and about 1861 he acquired from William and Frances
Thomas six hundred acres near Ward's Creek, south of Baton Rouge, that
became Windrush Plantation. The Thomas family had settled on Ward's
Creek in 1812 adjacent to land owned by John Thomas and fronting on the
Mississippi River. Pike's purchase included all improvements, machinery and
farming implements for $9,334, plus one slave, thirty-five-year-old Nathan.[10]

William Stephen Pike became a leading businessman in Baton Rouge; in
the 1850s he developed Pike's Row, a large office building complex built to
resemble the old army fort's pentagon barracks, on the north side of Florida
Street near the corner of Third Street. It housed several local businesses.
About the same time, Pike built a combined residence and commercial
building on Third Street to house a branch of the Louisiana State Bank
of New Orleans. He also owned other properties, such as Pike's Fireproof
Warehouse on the corner of Front and Laurel Streets, and was involved in
banking and mercantile businesses with several partners. He and partners Jean
Martial Lapeyre and Alexander Brother founded the private banking firm of

VIEW OF BATON ROUGE, LOUISIANA.

A bustling Baton Rouge welcomes Mississippi River flatboats and steamboats. *Courtesy of "Ballou's Drawing Room Companion," May 12, 1855.*

Pike, Lapeyre and Brother in 1836, with offices in New Orleans and Baton Rouge. Lapeyre served as president of the Louisiana State Bank from 1855 to 1866. About 1872, Pike married Mary Ann Huguet (circa 1844–1905), the sister of another business partner, Adolphe Hiram Huguet (born 1837). Pike and Huguet owned Baton Rouge and New Orleans property together.[11]

Family papers indicate that William Stephen Pike allowed his niece, Emma Gertrude Barbee (1836–1905), and her husband, John Charles Burden (1833–1872), to live at Windrush Plantation after their marriage in 1856. The first of the Burdens to settle in Baton Rouge, John Charles had immigrated to the United States from the town of Whitney, Oxfordshire, England, in the Cotswolds, which was near the Windrush River. It was they who named the plantation Windrush, because it reminded Burden of his English home. As an agent for an English importer, he traveled throughout the Caribbean and Southern United States, locating and purchasing various products and materials for shipment to England. The Pike, Lapeyre and Brother Bank engaged in foreign currency exchange and was the type of company an agent like Burden would have utilized. Socially, Burden could have been invited to Pike's home in New Orleans or Baton Rouge—as there he met his future wife, Emma.

John Charles Burden is listed as a merchant in the 1860 census. The 1870 census lists him as a farmer. During the Civil War and Reconstruction in Baton

The original Windrush Plantation house, sketched by Steele Burden. *Courtesy of the Burden Family Papers, LLMVC, LSU Libraries.*

Rouge, the family lived at Windrush Plantation, a difficult time in Louisiana, socially and economically. His estate at his death in 1872 at the age of thirty-eight was valued at only $2,634.50. He owned five mules, fifteen cows and heifers, thirty-eight acres of sugar cane, eight bales of cotton and 250 bushels of corn.[12]

In the 1880s, the Steele family, another group integral to the story of Windrush Plantation, arrived in Baton Rouge. Oliver Brice Steele (1844–1919), more commonly known as O.B., was born in Henderson, Kentucky. In 1861, O.B. enlisted in Kentucky's Fourth Infantry as a bugler. Although his unit fought in the Battle of Baton Rouge, O.B. was ill and missed the battle. However, he distinguished himself throughout the war and was promoted to captain. After the war, Captain O.B. Steele returned to Louisiana. He joined T.B. Hotchkiss in a mercantile business in Morehouse Parish, Louisiana, in January 1866. About the first of January 1869, he moved to New Orleans to work in John Gauche's wholesale dry goods business. By December 1869, O.B. had moved to Quachita City, near Monroe, Louisiana, where he met and married Juliet Mattie Parks in 1870 or 1871.[13]

Captain Steele was a successful farmer and merchant in Union, Morehouse and Quachita Parishes in northeastern Louisiana and was

J'apprecirais votre support pour la

NOMINATION DEMOCRATIC

COMME

Auditeur de L'Etat

Cordialement,

O. B. STEELE.

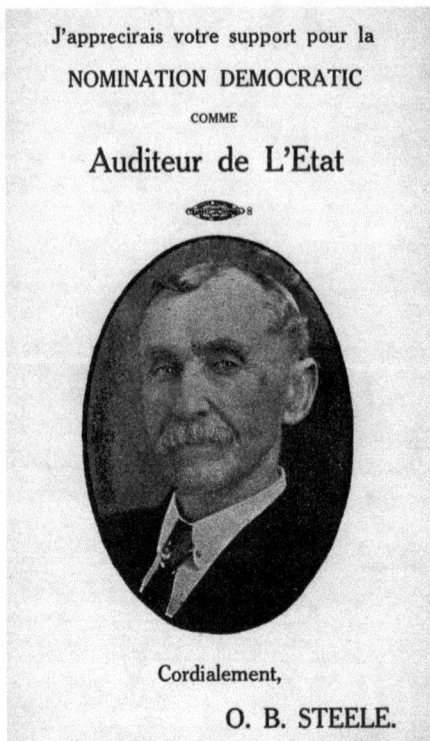

O.B. Steele appealed to French-speaking citizens of Louisiana when campaigning for state auditor in 1888. *Courtesy of the Burden Family Papers, LLMVC, LSU Libraries.*

elected state auditor in 1884. Reelected auditor in 1888 and elected state treasurer in 1892, Steele and family made Baton Rouge their home and became active and valuable members of the community. They lived at the corner of North and Third Streets in downtown Baton Rouge. He was an organizer of the Istrouma Social Club and a member and officer of the Baton Rouge St. James Lodge No. 47 Fraternal Order of Masons and the Knights of Pythias.[14]

O.B. was prominent in the early banking establishments of Baton Rouge. In 1889, he (as vice-president) and W.J. Knox (as president) established the Bank of Baton Rouge, with offices on Third Street. In 1916, O.B. resigned from the Bank of Baton Rouge to head a new bank that combined the Mercantile Bank and the Capital City Bank. He was also the president of the Louisiana Fire Insurance Company; the Zadok Reality Company, which oversaw his substantial Baton Rouge property; and an officer of the Suburban Electric Company.[15]

O.B. and Juliet Steele's oldest child, daughter Ollie Brice Steele (1870–1958), married the youngest son of John Charles and Emma Burden, William

O.B. Steele with bank partners on the steps of the Bank of Baton Rouge. *Courtesy of the Rural Life Museum Collection, MSS 3151, LLMVC, LSU Libraries.*

Customers inside the Bank of Baton Rouge. *Courtesy of the Rural Life Museum Collection, LLMVC, LSU Libraries.*

Ollie Brice Steele in her
elaborate wedding gown.
*Courtesy of the Burden Family
Papers, LLMVC, LSU Libraries.*

Stephen Pike Burden (1870–1925), who was born at Windrush Plantation. Their wedding on July 7, 1895, was the last one held in the old St. James Episcopal Church building. Their children were Ione Easter Burden; William Stephen Pike Burden Jr., who married Jeannette Monroe (1911–1970); and Ollie Brice Steele Burden. It was they who developed and gave to Baton Rouge the Rural Life Museum and Windrush Gardens. When interviewing Steele Burden in 1994, Kathy Grigsby commented that it seemed to her that the Burden family was "ahead of their times in their social outlook" and everything they did. Steele, in his usual modest manner, replied that he never thought that he or his family had done anything outstanding. To him they were ordinary working folks.[16]

William S. Pike Burden Sr., a graduate of LSU, was in the grocery and dry goods business. His stationery states that he was a dealer in "coal, stove and cord wood" and located in the Baton Rouge Police Jury building. He ran an unsuccessful campaign for election as the commissioner of public parks and streets for Baton Rouge but was elected city auditor/treasurer sometime after 1895, an office he held until his death.

William S. Pike Burden Sr. acquired title to Windrush Plantation in 1905. He began farming there and took the family out to visit on weekends. By 1921, the Burdens had moved permanently to Windrush Plantation. In 1925, William S. Pike Burden Sr. died of heart failure at age fifty-five. W.P. Burden's funeral service was held in the new St. James Episcopal Church building and his burial at Magnolia Cemetery. W.P.'s stature in Baton Rouge was shown by those participating in his ceremonies: Governor Henry L. Fuqua read the Masonic ritual at the grave, and pallbearers included Baton Rouge mayor Wade H. Bynum, as well as a number of well-known local businessmen.[17]

After William S. Pike Burden Sr.'s death, the husband of Ollie's sister Mayme, Dr. Lester James Williams (1882–1951), became a father figure to the family. He and Mayme married in 1906. From 1927 to 1946, Williams served as the chief of staff at Our Lady of the Lake Hospital. Everyone, family and residents of Baton Rouge, referred to him not by his given name but simply as "Doctor." Doctor aided Ollie and her children in many ways. He advised Ollie and Ione on investments and helped Pike Jr. to start his own printing business. Upon his death in 1951, Ione said that "for so many years all of us have looked upon Doctor as the head of the family and his passing is a very deep loss to us all."[18]

The Steeles moved from Quachita Parish to Baton Rouge, but Miss Ollie and her siblings maintained ownership of land in the northern parish. Some

Lester and Mayme Steele Williams enjoying the Windrush Gardens. *Courtesy of the LSU Rural Life Museum and Windrush Gardens.*

friends urged the family to sell parcels. However, Miss Ollie and brother, O.B. Steele Jr. (1895–1949), saw the benefits of keeping the Quachita land, including Morehouse Point Place, and land in Calcasieu Parish. About 1912, O.B. told her that the Independent Oil and Gas Company was anxious to run a pipeline through the Quachita property, as well as buy additional gas from the well on their property. He felt that it would be profitable and beneficial. Oliver B. Steele Jr. was the purchasing agent for Gulf State Utilities Company and lived in Baton Rouge at 1246 Convention Street with his wife, Nan Martin Steele. Unfortunately, Miss Ollie lost her trusted brother-advisor when O.B. Jr. died of a heart attack in May 1949. His funeral was also held at St. James Episcopal Church, although the interment was conducted at Roselawn Cemetery.[19]

OLLIE BRICE STEELE BURDEN (1870–1958)

One can speculate that the Steeles chose to name their daughter after her father because they were not certain that a male child and potential namesake would be born to them, nor that the child would live a long life due to the high rate of infant mortality in 1870 Louisiana. Miss Ollie, as she came to be known, not only lived a long life but also became a Baton Rouge civic leader, family mentor, cattle rancher and farmer, expert gardener and unique mother in that she taught her children through allowing them independence and through her participation in their interests.[20]

When the Steele family settled in Baton Rouge in 1885, fifteen-year-old Ollie entered Burritt's Institute for Girls located near Third Street. Her brothers attended Magruder's School for Boys. She took dancing at Lipod's Dancing Academy on Church Street in the former Washington Fire Company House Number One near Burritt's. She was well known for her piano solos at the yearly musical recitals held at the Mayer Hotel at Lafayette and Main. Ollie enjoyed her girls' Euchre Club as well.[21]

Colleges were not easily available to someone like Ollie Brice Steele, so her education was limited, and while she didn't push her three children to do anything they didn't want to do, she was an avid reader who instilled curiosity in them. Ollie was very popular and courted by a number of Baton Rouge's young men, including LSU cadet William Stephen Pike Burden. On each New Year's Day, many local girls would spend the day with Ollie at her parents' home. Boys would drop in and leave their "calling cards." Ollie and some of her friends became souvenir-lovers and retained their visitors' cards for many years. In 1955, she still had a calling card from her future husband received on one of those New Year's visits.[22]

Louisiana State University played a social role for Baton Rouge families. Even if their children did not attend LSU, they, like Ollie, could participate in events. The first Field Day, eventually known as Military Day, was held on May 13, 1893. As was traditional at other military schools, cadet companies had female sponsors. Ollie was appointed by Captain Dunbar Newell to be the first sponsor for Cadet Company B, one of four companies that existed at LSU. The last LSU dance of the school year was held on each Fourth of July. Ollie stated that they danced until sunrise, and then the girls would throw the long trains of their evening gowns over their arms and walk with the boys from the university down to the Old City Market four blocks away for coffee and doughnuts, after which the boys would walk them home. W.S. Pike Burden became Ollie's escort, and they were married in 1895. In 1896, their first child, Ione Easter Burden, was born, followed by Pike in 1898 and Steele in 1900.[23]

Miss Ollie and her peacocks at Windrush Plantation. *Courtesy of the LSU Rural Life Museum and Windrush Gardens.*

Ollie, Pike Sr. and their children were fond of visiting Windrush Plantation. A trip from their home on College Avenue in Spanish Town in downtown Baton Rouge out to the plantation took an all-day horse-and-buggy trip over dirt roads and trails that would become Perkins Road and Essen Lane, two future main thoroughfares of the city. Pike Sr.'s father had taken his family to live at Windrush during the Civil War and afterward. When his father died in 1872, the family (Pike Sr., his mother, his three sisters and his two brothers) moved to Third Street, probably to live in a house built by great-uncle William S. Pike, his namesake. Pike Sr. and Ollie made the decision to return to live at Windrush Plantation in 1921 to raise cattle and farm.

After the death of her husband Miss Ollie worked hard to keep the Windrush Plantation together for her family. Although she knew little about cattle, she got into the cattle business with a small herd of "common" cattle that she bred and sold. She also allowed tenant farmers to live and farm there. Ten tenant famer houses were built and rented out, with a small plot of land each. With the money earned from cattle raising and rents from tenant farmers, she kept Windrush Plantation in the family.[24]

Miss Ollie and her children were a close-knit group, developing some unusual and personal family traditions, such as Pike Jr.'s Mothers' Day celebration. Each year, he and a friend would circle low over the house in Pike's airplane and drop a box containing candy or roses for the women to catch. The family joked that the box most often landed in the trees or bushes instead of where they could catch it. Pike had learned to fly in World War I and built his own airfield at Windrush Plantation, which was used by local flyers for many occasions. Miss Ollie was known for loving traditions. The cake knife from her 1895 wedding became one of those traditions. It was presented by Miss Ollie to every subsequent bride in the family to use on her wedding day.[25]

Miss Ollie, a petite eighty-three-year-old, was still "independent and lively," reported Annabelle Armstrong in an article for the *Baton Rouge State Times* in 1955. Once, when she wanted to see the spring flowers in Baton Rouge, a friend and fellow flyer with Pike picked her up in his airplane and flew low over city to show her the blooming flowers and trees. She also stayed active with LSU Delta Kappa Gamma Sorority functions, many of which were held at her home, and never missed a performance of the Baton Rouge Symphony Orchestra. Gardening, said daughter Ione, was her principal interest. Ollie, along with Steele, was responsible for the beauty of Windrush Gardens. Every morning, she was found working in her ten-acre gardens or checking the water for her own herd of cattle. She had friends from all over the world send her small gifts, such as cups and saucers, and she kept them all.[26]

WILLIAM STEPHEN PIKE BURDEN JR. (1898–1965)

The second child of Ollie Brice Steele and William S. Pike Burden Sr. became known as Pike. William Stephen Pike Burden Jr.'s baptismal certificate was signed on September 15, 1898, at a ceremony in St. James Episcopal Church in Baton Rouge, with his grandmothers as his sponsors. William Stephen Pike Burden Jr. was named for his father and his granduncle, William Stephen Pike. He lived all his life in Baton Rouge—except for a few years in the military air corps during World War I—attended but did not graduate from LSU and became a printer and publisher after the war.[27]

Pike and younger brother Steele were known around Baton Rouge for childhood pranks. An old friend, J.S. Herget, wrote in 1958 that the first time he had met the Burden boys they were trying to break out a streetlight in front of his house by throwing rocks at it. Herget also remembered that Pike did "everything but study in school" and got thrown out of the public high school so he had to attend St. Vincent's Academy, known as Brothers'. He went back and forth between the public high school and Brothers' until he was finally able to graduate. Herget believed it was only through the influence of the Brothers of St. Vincent's that Pike was allowed to enter LSU. According to Herget, Pike as a printer was forgetful about customers' orders. Many times, he had been one of the customers whose orders Pike forgot. Still, they remained good friends.[28]

Pike and his wife, Jeanette Monroe, built an antebellum-style home at Windrush Plantation in 1940 across the lane from the almost ninety-year-old house in which Miss Ollie, Miss Ione and Mr. Steele lived. Pike was a charter member of the Baton Rouge Rotary Club formed in 1918, and he eventually served as vice-president and president in the early 1950s. He founded the Rotarian Crippled Children's Fund and the Rotarian scholarship for LSU music students. Pike also donated land to establish local parks.

Pike's business was publishing and printing, Pike Burden, Inc., but his two favorite activities were magic and flying. Pike was an amateur magician, participating in social organizations geared to philanthropic work for children and the elderly. He performed to Baton Rouge civic and social groups in the 1940s and throughout the state to such groups in 1950s and 1960s. He also arranged for celebrity magicians to come to perform in town. His personal archives are filled with letters thanking him for his performances. His stage name was "Pike the Magician."[29]

Pike once said that his magic hobby kept him sane while dealing with the pressures associated with his publishing and printing business. Pike enjoyed

"Pike the Magician."
Courtesy of the Burden Family Papers, LLMVC, LSU Libraries.

performing magic for children and LSU students. He liked to be around kids, he said, because they were fun and adults were not, for they had forgotten "how to be young." Pike explained in a memoir how he came to love magic and find its value as a healing art for himself and others. He developed an interest in model railroads, but during World War II he could not get new parts and pieces for his collection. Instead, he began to study about and attempt some magic tricks. While at the Mayo Clinic in Minnesota for a checkup, he practiced the "little bit of magic he already knew" and drew an appreciative crowd of other patients. His doctors encouraged him to learn more because it was a good way for him to slow down and relax. They also asked him to plan to entertain the patients when he came to the Mayo Clinic for his yearly checkups. Pike discovered that a Mayo Clinic laboratory employee was also a professional magician. He taught Pike, and they did some shows together.[30]

After learning to fly during World War I, Pike became a great supporter of modern aviation in Louisiana. He served on the Baton Rouge City-Parish Airport Commission, which developed out of the Downtown and Ryan

"Pike the Flying Colonel" and friends on the airfield at Windrush Plantation. *Courtesy of the LSU Rural Life Museum and Windrush Gardens.*

(north Baton Rouge) Airports. When Pike retired from the commission in 1957, the president of Delta Airlines appointed him a "Flying Colonel," an honor presented to him by Baton Rouge mayor Jack Christian in a public ceremony. Numerous other awards for public service related to aviation development were given to Pike. He helped organize the local chapters of the Civil Air Patrol, the Fellowship of Quiet Birdmen and the Baton Rouge Chapter of the National Aeronautics Association.[31]

Pike was also an amateur artist whose work turned up in some unusual places. Because of a lung injury, Pike sometimes went to Our Lady of the Lake Hospital near his Windrush Plantation home. A bed in the pediatrics ward was the only one available in 1957 when he required hospitalization. While staying, he became bored, and with the help of an artist friend they painted a mural on the wall to entertain the children also staying in the ward. Then he funded materials for a playroom near the mural and drew a design for it. But to apologize for his artistic "jokes," he donated funds for the hospital to buy an incubator for babies.[32]

Pike was a small, wiry man with gray hair and twinkling blue eyes. *Courtesy of the Burden Family Papers, LLMVC, LSU Libraries.*

Pike Burden was named Baton Rouge's Outstanding Citizen of the Year (1960–61) and received the Golden Deeds Award. A testimonial presented at the Golden Deeds banquet gave a succinct but thorough description of Pike Burden:

> *This small wiry man with grey hair and twinkling blue eyes, barely tips the scales at one hundred pounds—a nonconformist and a man who lives by his principles. If clothes make the man, he would be on the bottom of the list, thinks nothing of attending a formal affair in sports clothes. He gets by with this social error because it is expected of him. It is one of his trademarks. His half million dollar printing business started in the men's room of a local firm. He printed many orders by hand and finally had enough money to invest in a small printing press. Like a small boy he owns a priceless art collection, but also loves any dime store toy and displays such side by side. He has two great hobbies: magic and miniature railroads. He is known only as Pike like Liberace or Lafayette. Pike is truly a self made man, who spurned college and travel. He taught himself all there is to know about electronics and machinery and was also instrumental in building the first airport in this city.*[33]

Many stories about Pike are part of Baton Rouge folklore. Perhaps the best known is when Pike lost his driver's license for two weeks for illegal parking and other traffic violations. So he parked the car and went on with his deliveries by horse and buggy; when he needed to stop, he tied the horse to a parking meter. Another prankster, Dr. John Melton, who became minister of the First Presbyterian Church, once took the horse and buggy—for which Pike had him charged with horse rustling.[34]

IONE EASTER BURDEN (1896–1983)

Ione Easter Burden, the oldest child of Ollie Brice Steele and William Burden, was born on Easter, April 5, 1896, explaining why her grandmothers named her "Easter." Childhood stories about Ione Easter are few, probably because her brothers, Pike and Steele, were too mischievous for her to outdo them and gain notice. They all grew up in downtown Baton Rouge near the campus of Louisiana State University, which was located where the current Louisiana state capitol building stands now. Unlike her brothers, Ione enjoyed school and entered LSU in 1913, graduating with a bachelor's degree in English four years later. During her student years at LSU, Ione was an active member of the Delta Kappa Gamma Sorority and stayed involved with the sorority all her life, hosting parties and events at the Windrush Plantation house along with her mother. She served as editor in chief of the campus yearbook, the *Gumbo*, in 1917, was active in many theatre productions and was chosen as the most popular coed.[35]

Ione's first job after graduation was as the assistant registrar at LSU. From 1917 until 1926, this job set her career path. In 1926, she accepted the position of registrar at Louisiana Polytechnic Institute (now Louisiana Tech University) in Ruston, Lincoln Parish, in north Louisiana, working there until 1929. Later that year, Ione took a huge step away from family and friends when she moved to Williamsburg, Virginia, to work as the secretary to the Dean of the College of William and Mary. Promoted to assistant to the dean, Ione stayed at the College of William and Mary for four years.

On December 8, 1932, Ione resigned from the College of William and Mary because she had been offered a position by the president of Louisiana State University as the assistant to the dean of student affairs. Once back at LSU, Ione worked there until her retirement from the position of director of student activities in 1961 at age sixty-five. Steele felt that his sister had a successful life and a nice career at LSU. He and others saw her as one of the first liberated women they knew—a leader and an independent thinker.[36]

Ione was very much a behind-the-scenes person, however. She declined appointment to the Executive Committee of the Alumni Association in 1942 and also refused to be considered for appointment as dean of women in 1947, even though the resigning dean had recommended Ione as her successor. Ione wrote to supporters asking them not to recommend her for the position because she felt that the person named to the job should "have superior academic training, actual training in personnel work and Deaning [sic], and experience in handling students and assisting personnel."[37] In May 1947, a new dean of women at LSU was appointed, and in 1948, Ione was promoted to director of student activities.

As secretary to the dean of student affairs and later as director of student activities at LSU, Ione was responsible for setting the dates for all social and scholastic events without having conflicts among them. Despite what could have been an unpopular job, Ione was one of the "best liked and best known figures on campus." She also answered letters from anyone who had a question about LSU. "I've been at the University so long and have done so many different things that I always have a hard time when anyone asks me what I do."

Ione liked dealing with a variety of people, and that made her successful. "She is an attractive individual, with a competent air that inspires confidence, and many of the students come to her with their problems." Her office in the field house was a central hub for students, with yearly scheduling requests for hundreds of parties, plays, concerts and games. Ione found time to relax at her Windrush home by gardening with her mother and brother. She was also a stamp collector.[38]

Each year at LSU, Ione took on more responsibilities for student activities and university events. In August 1950, the university president appointed her chairman of the University Publications Committee, responsible for compiling and editing all publications issued by the campus. This was added to her regular duties, he said, because Ione and her staff had done such an excellent job the past year on the student guide.

In 1959–60, when LSU celebrated the centennial of its founding, Ione was appointed chairman of the Subcommittee on Open Houses to coordinate an event in April 1960, dedicating seven new buildings. She was also active in volunteer activities in Baton Rouge, not only with Delta Kappa Gamma Sorority but also with Phi Kappa Phi, the Our Lady of the Lake Hospital Board and as an organizer of the Greater Baton Rouge

Miss Ollie (center), with daughter Ione to her right and a group of LSU military sponsors. *Courtesy of the Burden Family Papers, LLMVC, LSU Libraries.*

YWCA. In addition to many other activities, Ione served on the Inaugural Day Committee to plan the events for the inauguration of a new Louisiana governor in May 1944.[39]

Ione's hard work and the family propensity to heart ailments affected her on December 26, 1957, when she had a heart attack. Her favorite aunt, Mayme Steele Williams, had died a month before on November 24, 1957. Unfortunately, an even sadder event for Ione, Pike and Steele occurred on November 17, 1958, when their mother, Miss Ollie, died. Ione struggled to recover from these events, but ten days after her mother's death she became severely ill again with shingles and only slowly recovered in the fall of 1959.[40]

On July 1, 1961, Ione retired from LSU. Those who had worked with Ione appreciated her. Helen Gordon wrote to her on June 30, 1966:

> *I can't complete my work as Dean of Women without this note of THANKS to you for all you have meant to me since I arrived on the job August 1, 1947. I could never have made it without you, because you have been a wonderful inspiration, advisor and "prop." I shall always be grateful to you for everything you've done for me and most of all for your friendship.[41]*

Ione and colleagues at work planning student activities at LSU. *Courtesy of the Burden Family Papers, LLMVC, LSU Libraries.*

Family papers abound with letters from Ione to various family members, most often to her mother, Miss Ollie. Ione loved to travel, and her letters home describe her trips and adventures. In May 1922, she received her first passport in order to travel to England, Belgium, Italy, Switzerland, France, Holland and Germany. She traveled extensively with friends and family members to Europe and throughout the United States. A few months after she retired, Ione and several friends were on a trip to New York City for the holidays.

Letters from Steele—just signed "S"—are less common but always humorous. He wrote to Ione during August 1950, while she and Aunt Mayme were in the Blue Ridge Mountains, on LSU Operation and Maintenance Department stationery, noting that he finally had a yard man, Albert Raby. Raby and other workers were getting Windrush cleaned up like it hadn't been for years. Steele brought Ione up-to-date on town and university happenings:

The Gianellonis had their oil well celebration last Sunday—I'm told— with much success. Champagne for the aristocracy and all the red whiskey the common people could drink. S.J. made a lengthy speech after which he presented $300 watches to those most responsible for the well's success. Things are quiet on the campus, with Farm Week over. We've just about picked up the last of the pop bottles—abandoned girdles, shoes etc. Pike's performance was appreciated.[42]

Ione, too, had a sense of humor. From Williamsburg in June 1931, she wrote to Mama that her friends were trying to teach her how to cook. Ione discovered that kitchens could be improved with modern appliances. "With a frigid-aire life is worth living. Get one if you can afford it as it is cheaper to run than to buy ice." Ione always managed a shared laugh at Steele's expense. When the president of LSU announced his retirement in February 1960, the public seemed surprised. Ione said that to the family the president's "action did not come as a surprise because Steele, who seems never to hear or see anything, misses nothing!"[43]

Ione continued her travels while working at the College of William and Mary. She had the opportunity to attend the inauguration of President Herbert Hoover in March 1929. After the inauguration, Ione wrote to her mother that she had ridden in the parade in Louisiana senator Ransdell's car because Governor Huey Long had not attended. Ione's group sat on the president's stand, and it rained throughout the entire speech and parade. She said that President Hoover gave the people a good show and never once pulled up the top of his car during the rain-drenched parade.[44]

Ione always stayed in touch with Baton Rouge friends, writing to them about her adventures, what she was learning about university administration and her hopes for the future. Ione told them that she hoped they could spend a summer together in England but that she ran "around too much to save any money." Eventually, Ione planned to return to Baton Rouge and maybe go back to LSU and get a master's degree. She felt confident that she could find a good job because she knew her recommendations from the College of William and Mary administrators would be strong, but she was concerned about finding a job that was interesting to her.[45]

Ione was sensitive to the historic preservation activity she saw as she traveled, and she was always interested in the gardens. Her letters describe in great detail the gardens and houses of George Washington, George Mason and President Jefferson's Monticello. She told Miss Ollie that even though she had been to Monticello at all times of the year, she was not sure which she thought was most beautiful but that certainly the spring was the "most alluring." "Can you imagine those beautiful mountains covered with dogwood and red bud and all of the trees in their spring attire? I would not take anything for the trip," she stated after a trip to Winchester and Port Royal, Virginia. From these trips, she sent Miss Ollie and Steele plants to grow at Windrush Plantation in the gardens.[46]

By the time Ione went to live in Williamsburg, Virginia, she had spent a lifetime with her mother and Steele and had continued their amazing love of nature and history and the preservation of both. Ione arrived in Williamsburg in 1929, soon after the Rockefeller Foundation began a restoration of the village. Ione believed that Steele would be thrilled to see what was being done in Williamsburg. Although she invited him to visit many times, it is unclear if he ever went there to visit Ione and see the work at Williamsburg. She wrote to her old friend, former LSU president Thomas Boyd, that it was amazing to see what had been accomplished in the gardens there, with blooming plants and huge trees such as hollies, beeches and elms brought in from the surrounding areas and planted where they were needed. One day, a house being restored would have no garden, and within a week there would be a garden that appeared as if it had always been there.[47]

When visiting Baton Rouge in August 1931, Ione told a newspaper reporter that the Rockefeller Project at Williamsburg was to restore the town to its pre–Revolutionary War physical setting—buildings as well as gardens and shops. Ione watched the developments as old houses were taken down, their foundations were strengthened and the original nails were straightened out and used to rebuild the houses. Ione would support Steele as he began to restore historic buildings for the Rural Life Museum in 1970.

St. Alban's Chapel Episcopal Student Center on the LSU campus was a favorite of Ione's. In memory of Lester and Mayme Williams, Ione paid for the creation and installation of a stained-glass window there, and after her mother's death in November 1958, she purchased one in her mother's memory as well. Ione was generous to other local organizations, as were her brothers. Throughout the Burden Family Papers are many letters thanking them for their philanthropy. To the LSU Delta Kappa Gamma Sorority House, Ione gave funds for a book collection in 1967. Later that year, she made donations to the LSU Library, the Baton Rouge Music Club and the LSU Anglo-American Art Museum. In 1975, Ione helped the Foundation for Historical Louisiana with funds for the restoration of the Magnolia Mound Plantation House. She also established two LSU scholarships in memory of her uncle, Dr. Lester J. Williams.[48]

Throughout her life, Ione remained involved in community activities. *Courtesy of the Burden Family Papers, LLMVC, LSU Libraries.*

In 1960, Pike, his wife Jeanette, Ione and Steele explored the idea of donating their land known as Windrush Plantation to the State of Louisiana. To this end, they created and incorporated the nonprofit Burden Foundation to "accept and administer gifts, donations, grants and bequests, and manage those and make donations to others; promote and conduct activities; assist in furnishing of physical facilities; give scholarships for the above purposes; and provide for the general educational and recreational welfare through parks, zoos, and facilities." The main responsibility of the Burden Foundation was to ensure that the recipient of Windrush Plantation fulfilled its contractual obligations of the act of donation. In 1964, they considered giving the land to Louisiana State University, stipulating what it could and could not be used for.[49]

However, by October 1965, the Burdens had not made a final decision, and the Burden Foundation attorney, Alvin B. Rubin, requested that Governor John McKeithen appoint an appropriate expert to make recommendations for the use of the Windrush Plantation if it were donated to the state. Rubin explained that for a number of years LSU had been permitted to use portions of Windrush Plantation for agricultural experimental projects and that thirty acres of the plantation had already been donated to Our Lady of the Lake Hospital. This resulted in a response from Louisiana State Parks and Recreation Commission director Lamar Gibson in November 1965. Gibson told Rubin that the commission had designed plans to make Windrush Plantation into a naturalistic state park. However, less than a year later, the Burdens designated LSU as the recipient of the gift of the land.

Rubin informed Ione on August 23, 1966, that he was happy that efforts regarding the Windrush Plantation donation had reached a conclusion. The act of donation to LSU was recorded in the East Baton Rouge Parish Clerk of Court's office on October 7, 1966. The Burden Foundation Board of Directors reported at its May 10, 1967 meeting that they were generally happy with the research projects being carried out by LSU at Windrush Plantation. Each subsequent year, the board of directors seemed pleased with LSU. Steele stated at its meeting on May 12, 1970, that he felt that LSU had done a "commendable job in the time and with the funds available for the Windrush project." Also at this meeting, Steele reported that he had been successful in locating some antebellum buildings for a museum dedicated primarily to rural nineteenth-century Louisiana life, to be developed at Windrush Plantation. In 1992, the final parcel of land, the last in a succession of tracts, was donated by the Burden Foundation to LSU, giving the complex a total of 440 acres.[50]

Before the Burdens embarked on the future donation of Windrush Plantation, they sought to aid a Baton Rouge institution in the development and building of a senior citizens retirement and long-term care facility on land at Windrush. Ione corresponded with St. James Episcopal Church officials and administrators of Our Lady of the Lake Hospital about such a project. By August 1963, the Burden Foundation had chosen to donate thirty acres to Our Lady of the Lake Hospital for a nonsectarian home for the aged, to be named the Ollie Steele Burden Manor. Ione, Pike and Steele would make the donations of land through the Burden Foundation.[51]

The Franciscan Missionaries of Our Lady, an affiliate of Our Lady of the Lake Regional Medical Center, established the Burden Memorial Hospital, Inc., as a nonprofit organization to oversee the home for the aged. Architect A. Hays Town of Baton Rouge, and friend of the Burdens, was chosen to design the buildings. Groundbreaking took place on September 15, 1964. The Ollie Steele Burden Manor opened in the spring of 1966.

On December 21, 1966, Sister Gertrude, the hospital administrator and Mother Superior, wrote to Ione and Steele thanking them for all of their gifts to the organization: vases, candlesticks, Miss Ollie's picture, occupational

Steele Burden: "All I ever was in my life was a yard man." *Courtesy of the LSU Rural Life Museum and Windrush Gardens.*

therapy supplies, saints' pictures and crucifixes, as well as a Christmas tree and a party for everyone at Thanksgiving. She looked forward to the park to be developed around the manor for which the Burdens had already donated a statue of St. Francis for the courtyard, an outdoor fountain, landscaping and a carillon.[52]

Ione and Steele were the recipients of numerous community, state and national awards for their own work and also for the work and gifts of the Burden family. Steele and Ione were presented a plaque from the American Institute of Architects in June 1974 for "their contributions in preserving the mementoes of the Southern way of life." They were awarded honorary degrees of doctor of cultural sciences for their service to the community and the university by LSU in 1975 for their donation of Windrush Plantation for agricultural research; Windrush Gardens, an eight-acre park of landscaped gardens; and the Rural Life Museum, "a complex of buildings and artifacts depicting eighteenth and nineteenth century Louisiana rural culture." In 1976, the Foundation for Historical Louisiana honored them for their preservation efforts throughout Baton Rouge. Then, in 1979, they were two of seven people to be honored as Baton Rouge Volunteer Activists of the Year.[53]

In 1980, when noted British museum authority Kenneth Hudson was asked to choose the top ten outdoor museums in the world, he included the Rural Life Museum. It was the only museum in the United States included. Hudson required that for a museum to receive the award it had to "make you feel better after you've been around it." In 1981, the Rural Life Museum was nominated by the Baton Rouge Area Convention and Visitor's Bureau for a Phoenix Award, given by the Society of American Travel Writers. The Rural Life Museum was selected for "outstanding work in the area of environmental or historic preservation." This was the first Phoenix Award ever given to a Louisiana recipient and one of only eight presented. In 1984, the Burdens were also honored with a medal from the Garden Club of America for work of national importance. Pike, his wife Jeanette, Ione and Steele Burden accomplished what their mother, Miss Ollie, had hoped. They preserved their home, Windrush Plantation, out of respect for their family heritage and made the world a better place through their actions.[54]

Chapter 2

"ALL I EVER WAS IN MY LIFE WAS A YARD MAN"

Ollie Brice Steele Burden (1900–1995)

The LSU Rural Life Museum and Windrush Gardens were inspired by Steele Burden, who was inspired by the beauty of nature, his ancestors' artistic spirits and the need to do good work. A whimsical, astute, perceptive and logical person, he was also modest and shy. Steele always stated, "All I ever was in my life was a yard man, only." However, his landscaping pursuits had a lasting effect on Baton Rouge. His legacy to the city was gardens, trees and the Rural Life Museum and Windrush Gardens.[55]

Ollie Brice Steele Burden (1900–1995) was the namesake of his grandfather, Oliver Brice Steele, and his mother, Ollie Brice Steele Burden. He was known around the world, however, as simply Mr. Steele, in the Louisiana tradition of addressing the elders of a community. When the family lived at the corner of Third and North Streets in downtown Baton Rouge, Steele attended St. Vincent's Academy of the Catholic Church on North Street. During 1915–16, he studied forestry at LSU but dropped out after a few semesters. Too young for military service in World War I, he joined the Student Army Training Corps at LSU, and he volunteered for service in World War II. Because of his experience with landscaping, he was assigned to the Camouflage Division of the Army Eighty-fourth Engineering Battalion in 1942 and was stationed at Camp Livingston near Alexandria, in central Louisiana, for eighteen months. Steele was awarded a state certification in landscape gardening, but he never completed a college degree.[56]

Steele appeared at the age of three (center) on a float for the Fireman's Day Parade. *Courtesy of the Rural Life Museum Collection, LLMVC, LSU Libraries.*

Steele's love of beauty, especially in nature, took hold in 1921 when the family moved to Windrush Plantation. He learned about the joy of beautiful things, in nature and in art, from his grandfather, Captain O.B. Steele, an amateur painter and art collector. O.B. collected art for his home and also created sketches and paintings, which he displayed among his collections. Steele spent his formative years around O.B., from whom he inherited artistic abilities. As a young man, Steele began to notice the colors and fragrances of plants. On Laurel Street, in downtown Baton Rouge, he first saw azaleas and wanted to learn everything about them. Live oak trees, however, became his favorite plant. He often stated, "The finest thing to come out of the earth is the live oak tree."[57]

Steele's father farmed, raised cattle and grew cotton and corn at Windrush Plantation. Steele said that his father raised corn to feed the mules and raised the mules to plow and cultivate the corn. Windrush Plantation was of little monetary value when Steele's parents received it, but the land was developed, gradually, through their work. The old house built about 1856 consisted of a porch half as wide as the house, which everyone loved.

Steele admitted that when he was about twenty-six years old he wasn't doing much in life, so he started trying to do something with the house and

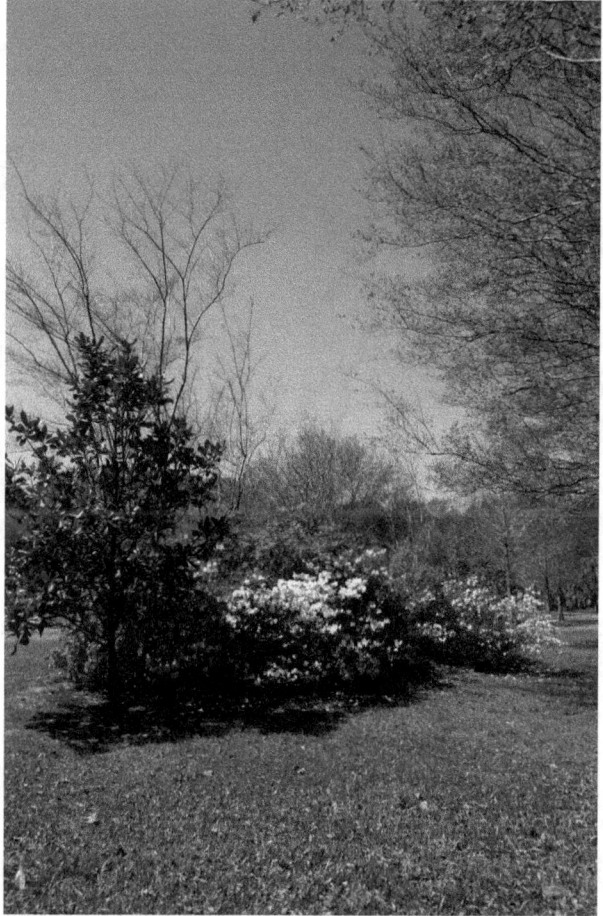

Steele's love of azaleas began when he was a child, and they appear again and again in his gardens. *Courtesy of Nancy N. Colyar.*

area around it to help his mother. His interest in planting and landscaping started then, but he began to use the knowledge he had already gained about plants such as azaleas. In the gardens of Windrush, Steele constructed a brick garden house in 1926 that served as his art studio, where he sketched, painted and sculpted. The signature plant of Mr. Steele, the live oak, was first used by him in gardens around the studio. In 1995, over four hundred oak trees were counted on the Windrush Plantation (known by then as the Burden Research Center), and many of them were planted by Steele. Over the years, the Burden family would hold many parties in the gardens and the studio. The design of the little studio was so popular that it was replicated in many landscapes throughout Baton Rouge, sometimes by Steele and sometimes by others. Steele, in his usual modest way, could not

Steele's sketch of his brick garden cottage, fashioned after a double pen slave cabin. *Courtesy of the Burden Family Papers, LLMVC, LSU Libraries.*

understand why people wanted to copy it, as "it was just a little getaway for me and a studio."[58]

Windrush Gardens began near the house when Steele applied his artistic ability to a former pigpen site and designed it into his first formal garden. A round, concrete pond with waterlilies and a pouring fountain centered the open lawn that ended with beds edged by mondo grass and containing some of Steele's favorite plants, including azaleas, bananas, banana shrubs, camellias, crape myrtles, gingers, sweet olives and wax-leaf ligustrum shrubs. These plants, plus oak trees, appeared again and again in Steele Burden–designed gardens, as they are so well adapted to the Louisiana climate. Other trademarks were pea gravel paths radiating from the center of the garden and statuary throughout.

For this first garden, Steele chose a statue that was a Baton Rouge landmark. The iron statue had once stood in a parterre garden on Third Street downtown behind Pike's Hall (built by Steele's ancestor, William Stephen Pike), which was home to the Elks' Club. Stories say it was the first outdoor sculpture in Baton Rouge, but the exact date it was acquired is unknown. Steele's father found it in a refuse pile about 1918 and took it to Windrush Plantation. On this early work, Steele commented that it was a time of getting the place landscaped and developing his interest in gardening. Miss Ollie also developed her love of gardening then.[59]

Traveling to the formal gardens of Europe as a young man heightened Steele's innate artistic sensibilities. He found, especially in Italy, symmetrically designed beds in garden rooms highlighted with statuary, water features and other garden ornamentation and connected by *alleés*. He continued to travel to Europe, Latin America and South America to absorb the beauty of the gardens and surround himself with beautiful plants and decoration. Steele's style emphasized the "green garden," based on the use of permanent shrubs and trees for color and texture rather than flowers. He left space to insert seasonal flowing plants among the shrubs and trees enclosing the garden rooms. He claimed that he never considered his work to be one style of garden or another—neither formal nor informal—but rather just attractive and full of beauty. Steele gave this sense of garden style to Baton Rouge.[60]

The second formal garden at Windrush was created by Steele in the 1930s near the first and behind the house. In the 1940s, he developed an

Statues collected by Steele are found throughout Windrush Gardens. *Courtesy of the LSU Rural Life Museum and Windrush Gardens.*

Baton Rougeans believe that Steele Burden was the first to use sugar kettles as garden features. *Courtesy of the LSU Rural Life Museum and Windrush Gardens.*

even larger area to the south of the others. He changed vegetable gardens into ovoid and circular garden rooms surrounded by shrub beds. Some of the rooms led the visitors to peek into adjoining garden rooms and follow pea gravel paths. Steele liked gardens with elements of seclusion. Each room incorporated niches for statues on brick pedestals—always an important element to his garden rooms. Other garden items came from local Baton Rouge landmarks, such as urns from the Garig House, which once stood where the River Center is now located downtown. He also liked to incorporate items from the Rural Life Museum collections, such as gaslights, benches, olive jars and sugar kettles. Baton Rougeans believe that Steele was the first landscape designer to make use of old sugar kettles as water features in gardens and lawns.[61]

Twenty-five acres were eventually designed into Steele Burden garden rooms. After he retired in 1970 from over forty years as LSU's landscaper, Steele spent the next two decades further developing the Windrush Gardens. LSU forestry students had planted a small grove of pine trees, and when they were almost mature, Steele created among them informal and irregular nature gardens and trails. Along with his trademark sculpture within the woodland setting, he had constructed two ponds to attract wildfowl, with

Man-made lakes at the Windrush Gardens attract waterfowl. *Courtesy of Nancy N. Colyar.*

benches and gazebos where visitors sat and viewed the ducks and geese. White, yellow and purple irises lined Steele's lake, which was inhabited by a pair of Australian black swans in addition to wood ducks that nested and raised their young in carefully placed boxes.[62]

Steele collected many plants, including saplings of native live oak, pine and other trees from the woods around the city or on Windrush Plantation. He planted many of those trees, especially the live oaks, in the Baton Rouge City Park, in neighborhoods, on the LSU campus or in the Windrush Gardens. From the local woods, he moved palmetto, yaupon, native irises and honeysuckle plants into formal gardens. For color, he added azaleas, crape myrtles, roses and camellias. For fragrance, he added sweet olive, gardenias, ligustrums and gingers. Few plant nurseries existed, so the woods were the only place to get the plants. Ione collected others on her travels and sent them to him.[63]

Steele tended the Windrush Gardens for almost seventy-five years, from the time he was twenty-one years old until his death at ninety-five. Steele Burden and the Burden Foundation's purpose for the Rural Life Museum and Windrush House and Gardens is that they "provide a tranquil setting where one might pause to appreciate natural beauty and a simpler way of life from times gone by."[64] *Baton Rouge Advocate* feature writer Sarah Sue Goldsmith drew a clear word picture of the Windrush Gardens in 1995 shortly after Steele's death:

> *Paths wound through the woods, leading nature lovers from one appealing vista to the next. Clusters of red berries hung like Christmas ornaments on ardesia shrubs, and cast-iron plants stood shoulder to shoulder like knights defending a castle. Palmetto fronds nodded in the light breeze. Indigofera lined the path by the hundreds, adding a touch of elegance with their delicate foliage and lacy pink flowers. The illusion of walking in a distant pastoral setting was complete.*[65]

CITY PARK WORK

"What Steele Burden loved most was creating gardens. His need to create aesthetically pleasing environments led him to become a landscape designer by trade. The first awareness that Baton Rouge citizens had of landscaping was …Victory Park." So notes a memorial to the veterans of World War I, located on Florida Street, where the Senator Russell B. Long Federal Court House now stands. Steele apprenticed for two years with the Chicago architectural landscape firm American Park Builders (APB) hired to create Victory Park.

When Steele was college age, there were only three landscape architecture schools in the United States and none near Baton Rouge. He felt that he could do better as an apprentice than as a student in a distant school far away from his home. In addition to work on the Victory Park, APB landscape architects designed a small park in the Hundred Oaks area and laid out Roselawn Cemetery. After that, APB was retained to design the Baton Rouge City Park and a golf course. Golf courses were a specialty of the American Park Builders. Steele worked with them first at the Hundred Oaks park and then at the Baton Rouge City Park.[66]

A description of the grounds of Victory Park shows that Steele learned much from the American Park Builders' landscape architects that he would utilize in his future work at Windrush Plantation, Baton Rouge City Park and LSU and in local neighborhood gardens. "Shell walks lead in a semi-circular way through attractive flower beds and tropical shrubbery…on the western side of the park is a large lawn…on the eastern side is a large water pool with small fish," and a rose garden was placed at the Tenth Street entrance.

Victory Park was dedicated on June 14, 1921, Flag Day and the 144th anniversary of the creation of the American flag.[67]

Steele often stated that he never wanted a full-time job for which he was obligated to be in the same place every day. However, in 1925 he began work for the Baton Rouge City Parks Department. This was the "first full-time, real job" that Steele accepted. "I didn't want to be pinned down to where I couldn't do as I pleased, and I've always done as I've pleased, as you well know," Steele told longtime friend Suzanne Turner in an oral history interview she conducted with him in 1993.

For a number of years, his supervisor was George Garig, of the socially prominent and wealthy Garig family, and Garig was not a kindly supervisor. Ione wrote to Steele in February 1931 that "I do so want you to finish the park," (the city park in south Baton Rouge) and hoped Garig would win a local election and leave the parks. Soon Steele took Garig's place as city parks superintendent. Steele Burden in his first years with Baton Rouge City

Cypress trees in the lake were some of the few trees that Steele did not plant in Baton Rouge City Park. *Courtesy of the LSU Rural Life Museum and Windrush Gardens.*

Park did much of the work himself, including climbing the trees to trim and prune them. He did what was needed to keep the trees healthy. He also found that the best way to train his helpers to properly take care of the trees and plants was to demonstrate the work himself. Later, Steele stated that he "planted practically all of the trees in City Park…except for a few cypress trees that were growing in the lake."[68]

Steele dreamed of a project to change the golf course in Baton Rouge City Park to a family area with walking paths. Because it was some of the only rolling, hilly land in Baton Rouge, he felt it would make a wonderful park, especially since fewer and fewer people played golf in the late twentieth century. Steele wanted to take the golf course land that parallels Dalrymple Road, with the little creek running through it, and make that into a small but typical Louisiana bayou with cypress, as it would have been naturally. He offered his own money to get it started, but the city determined to keep the Baton Rouge City Park Golf Course as it was. Steele actually wanted to convert all the land between Dalrymple Road and Stanford Road, south of downtown Baton Rouge, into a city park. In 2005, ten years after Steele's death, improvements were made in Baton Rouge City Park that he would have appreciated. Walking and bike trails, an improved art museum and tennis courts, a water feature and a dog park were added—yet the golf course remains.[69]

LSU WORK

In 1930, Louisiana State University professor James Broussard, who would later become dean of men, sought Steele's help to landscape the new campus. Louisiana State University's campus was moved from downtown to Highland Road in 1926, where the new buildings sat in former farm and cattle fields without trees or plants. An original design by the Olmsted brothers of Boston included lavish plantings throughout the campus. Their plan, however, was not followed since architect Theodore Link received the final design commission. Concentrating on the buildings, rather than the landscape, Link's plan resulted in beautiful buildings in a vacant landscape.

Campus administrators had hired E.A. McIlhenny of New Iberia to develop planting designs for some areas around the campus such as the outdoor Greek Theater. Although McIlhenny had completed the shrubbery and flowering plant design around it, Steele planted the trees that stood for over fifty years around the Greek Theater after he began working part time for LSU. Steele refused to take the LSU job full time because he still had work to do at the Baton Rouge City Park and already had promised to do work for homeowners throughout the city. However, after World War II, he worked full time for LSU and, like his sister Ione, worked for LSU until he retired.[70]

Baton Rouge City Park and the campus were surrounded by neighborhoods in which LSU faculty lived, and Steele had already landscaped many of their yards and gardens. He marked the LSU campus landscape with crape myrtles and live oak trees—familiar plants he had planted at those private homes. In addition to the trees planted on the campus center, he planted most of the live oaks that once lined Nicholson Drive, which up until the 1960s was one of the most desirable neighborhoods in Baton Rouge. Steele pointed out that he didn't plant all of the trees on the campus, even though people tended to credit him for them. A number of magnolia trees were there from when it was plantation and farmland. He did, however, begin the planting of Japanese magnolias around Pleasant Hall near the north entrance of the campus and in the triangles that border the Parade Grounds, giving a great bloom of color about February each year.

In 1931, the LSU Parade Grounds were still hayfields, and Steele had to cut them with a mower pulled by mules. The mower is now featured prominently at the Rural Life Museum. In the areas between buildings, he sought to have different combinations of color and smell, which he achieved with nandina and sweet olives or with ligustrum and camellias. Throughout the campus, Steele had patios and formal gardens installed. There were three patios behind the Faculty Club, as well as a formal garden. One patio is still there.[71]

Burden was very proud of work he did for the LSU president's house at the corner of Highland and Raphael Semmes Drive, across Highland Road from the Faculty Club and the Student Union. He installed a patio at the rear of the house within a formal garden that continued around the sides of the house. An arbor seating area was reached by a small secluded walk with nighttime lights. He also created a small roof garden in which the president's wife kept a variety of birds. Steele lamented that in 1993 all of this work was gone, torn out by those who followed him in landscaping the campus.[72]

While many of the original live oak trees planted by Steele Burden have died of natural causes or from storm damage, many hundreds are still standing and near one hundred years old. On the LSU campus, the Save an Oak endowment provides funding from donors to care for and preserve the oaks he planted. The money pays for daily maintenance and, when a

Azaleas and oak trees planted by Steele still grace the LSU campus. *Courtesy of Jim Zietz, LSU University Relations.*

tree dies, a replacement for it. Plaques in honor of donors or as memorials to others acknowledge those who love the trees as Steele did. I'd "like to take credit for every tree that God didn't plant."[73]

Steele retired from full-time work for LSU in 1970, but he still maintained an interest in the landscape work on university property. A small peninsula in the University Lake existed and was enlarged by dirt thrown up when the lake was dredged. It is across from the house at East Lakeshore Drive used as the home of LSU System presidents and then as the home of LSU chancellors.

In 1976, the LSU president kept two horses on the peninsula. Steele wanted the horses moved so that a primitive woodland might grow and attract birds. Steele asked Dudley Fricke, an assistant to the president, to encourage LSU to follow his suggestions. If the contour of the peninsula was changed to slope the edges down to the water, Steele argued, waterfowl would nest there. Fricke stated that Steele often became irritated because he did not push the LSU officials to accept the project as quickly as Steele wanted. They still became friends. Finally, in about three years, approval was obtained for Steele Burden to slope the edges of the land and plant oak trees and other native plants. Fricke believed that this helped, along with the abundant food supply in the lake, to lure white pelicans to visit the lakes for several weeks each winter.[74]

Fricke felt that Steele sought to develop projects such as the bird sanctuary and Rural Life Museum not because of personal vanity but because he felt that they were important to, and of lasting value to, society and culture. Steele wanted people to have access to nature and Louisiana's rural history. When Steele was cremated after his death in 1995, Fricke felt it "symbolically appropriate" that Steele's ashes were scattered on the Rural Life Museum land, thus returning him to nature. For Fricke, Steele's talent, commitment and life of compatibility with nature and Louisiana heritage were lasting memories.[75]

BEGINNINGS OF THE RURAL LIFE MUSEUM

Steele found an ally in LSU chancellor emeritus Cecil Taylor, who also felt it was important to preserve examples of Louisiana's agricultural way of life on plantations and small farms. Over the years, various people at the university had collected an assortment of folk art, antique tools and other nineteenth-century Louisiana cultural artifacts. Stored on racks on the ground floor of the football stadium, no one except Steele cared what would happen to this odd collection. He had a vision and a need to preserve it. Steele received permission from LSU and help from Taylor to move all of the items from the stadium out to his garden studio at Windrush Plantation. He combined these with other nineteenth-century items he had collected. Steele confirmed in an oral history interview that this "was the beginning of the museum. I agreed to take on the responsibility of taking care of those things."[76]

With some funding from LSU, a simple metal-roofed storage building was constructed to hold his and LSU's original collections. Formally established by LSU in 1970, the Rural Life Museum was managed only by Steele Burden for a number of years. Eventually, others were hired to help: Mike Jones, Johnny Cox, Dud Kennedy, Malcolm Tucker, John Dutton and George Raby. Mike Jones was hired in 1972 as the first employee and first curator.[77]

Lifelong Baton Rouge resident John Dutton became the second curator in 1974. Dutton stated that when he came to work at the museum in 1974,

In 2008, over sixty thousand people visited the Rural Life Museum and Windrush Gardens. *Courtesy of the LSU Photograph Collection, Office of Public Relations, UA, LSU Libraries.*

Steele had been collecting nineteenth-century farm items since the 1920s and, in 1972, purchased Dr. Ambrose Storck's collection of nineteenth-century furnishings. For the first fifteen years of Dutton's employment, his job description was to "do what needs doing." On weekends, John and Steele would drive along River Road looking for items and knocking on doors, offering to buy things. They were aided in the collecting by Malcolm Tucker and Al Jarreau. Dutton's job eventually evolved into training and overseeing student workers, collecting books for the museum's reference library, writing publicity materials and inventorying the collections of artifacts. Dutton trained and worked with the volunteer docents and took pride in the contributions made by them. Of Steele, he said, "Mr. Burden had precise spots for each piece of furniture." Each day, Dutton put any items that had been moved back where Steele wanted them. He said of Miss Ione that she "was quiet and stayed in the background, but when she spoke, I listened. She was very sharp, very strong and a fantastic businesswoman."[78]

At first, only the exhibit barn composed the museum, until Steele decided to add plantation buildings to the site, based on a living history museum he has visited in Copenhagen, Denmark. Always on the lookout for interesting items, Steele spied a row of houses along the River Road outside New

In 1970, slave cabins were moved from St. James Parish to the Rural Life Museum. *Courtesy of the LSU Photograph Collection, School of Architecture, UA, LSU Libraries.*

Orleans. He drove out into the field and found the owner, who reported that the buildings were former slave houses and were about to be burned down. Steele had long hoped to find an original slave cabin for the Rural Life Museum but had begun to think that none still existed. Steele pleaded for the owner to wait one more day while he sought help to move some of the buildings. He succeeded and also acquired from the same location the former overseer's house and a nearby church building. The buildings were the remains of Welham Plantation developed in the 1830s in St. James Parish near Hester, in south-central Louisiana.[79]

It was his sister, Ione, who provided the funding for Steele's dreams. He always gave her credit for this. He stated that he had spent thousands of his own dollars on the museum and that Ione has spent more. Unsure how she learned to invest money to make money, Steele admired her abilities: "Ione set up a foundation while she was alive. Ione accumulated money—I don't really know how because the family never had any money." He had planned to let the original 1856 Windrush House decay, despite the beautiful porch and the twenty-five acres of gardens designed by him, but Ione's foundation managers urged him to preserve the house and gave him $75,000 to do so, or as Steele said, "to prop the old house up again." But the museum was his

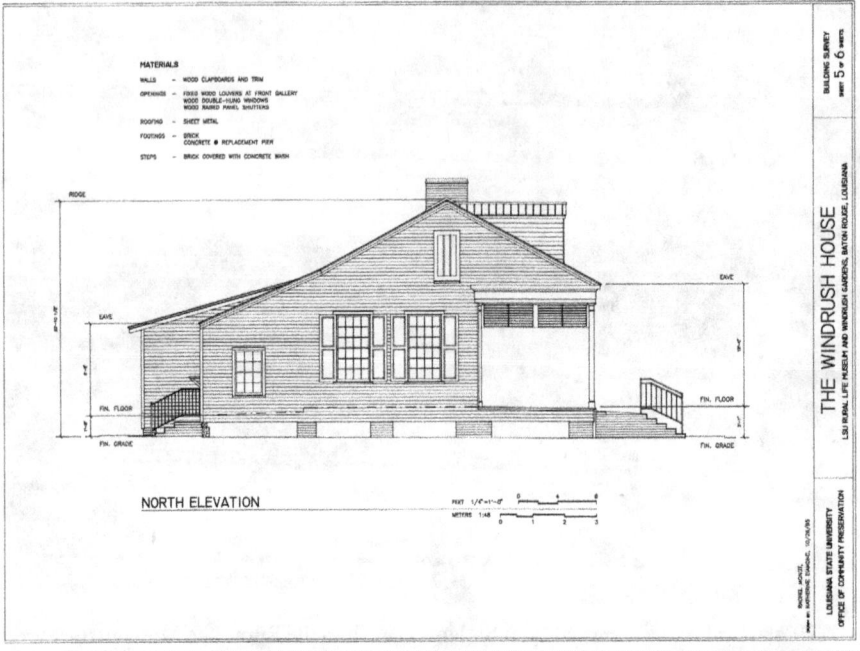

The original Windrush House, built about 1856, was restored by the Burdens. *Courtesy of the Louisiana Heritage Database, Historic American Buildings Survey, LA.*

The Windrush House was the family's favorite place to gather and hold community events. *Courtesy of the LSU Rural Life Museum and Windrush Gardens.*

own project, not Ione's and not the university's—only Steele's. "You know ideas, dreams are easy enough to come by, but accomplishments are another thing. You've got to plant the seeds."[80]

Steele worried that once he passed away the Rural Life Museum would cease to exist. He had been witness to Baton Rouge's proclivity to toss away the old, such as the first garden statue brought to Baton Rouge that his father has rescued from destruction. Steele also saw nineteenth-century buildings downtown demolished for parking lots and Victory Park closed. Luckily, LSU, the city, Ione's Burden Foundation and the good work of supporters kept the Rural Life Museum from being tossed away. Plus it has a productive future planned with the successful completion of the Whispers of Change campaign and the opening in 2010 of a new visitors' center. *Advocate* reporter Bob Anderson said of Steele, "Only the rarest of people will affect their communities as much as Burden, with acts that have graced not only his contemporaries, but future generations as well." Steele was an avid reader of philosophy, and a favorite statement of his was one by Erasmus: "For once you begin to take the human race too seriously, you will either lose your sense of humour or turn pious, and in either case you had much better be dead." Steele identified with the statement so much that he painted it on a door at the Rural Life Museum.[81]

Docents interpret nineteenth-century Louisiana rural life. *Courtesy of the LSU Photograph Collection, Office of Public Relations, UA, LSU Libraries.*

When asked what about the Rural Life Museum pleased him the most, Steele replied, "A person can come in and just sort of recall the past"—the true past. He was concerned that when tourists visited places like Natchez and New Orleans, they were never aware of what it took to build the plantation and city houses. By that, he meant slavery. At the Rural Life Museum, Steele strove to show what slavery was really like, with the slave quarters and the artifacts—chains, collars, shackles and whips—used on the slaves. Additionally, Steele appreciated seeing people come into the Rural Life Museum and Windrush Gardens out of the rush and noise of city traffic and be amazed to find "a serene, wooded area in the middle of a big town."[82]

WORK FOR PRIVATE HOMEOWNERS

There are many gardens around Baton Rouge that were designed by Steele Burden. One of the first was a courtyard surrounded by camellias for Anita and Payne Breazeale on Oleander Drive in the Garden District near the Baton Rouge City Park. Also in the Garden District Steele planted the live oaks in the center of Park Boulevard, the main thoroughfare of the area. He assisted Katherine Hill in the 1930s with her campaign to plant crape myrtles throughout the early neighborhoods of the Garden District, Hundred Oaks and others. One of his favorite private gardens was the rose garden he created for the Hart House at Magnolia Mound Plantation, including several small fish ponds. The gazebo Steele used in the garden came from its original location in the National Cemetery when the city discarded it. A Colonial Revival house at 2502 Dalrymple Drive was designed by the architects of the state capitol building—Weiss, Dreyfuss and Sieferth—for Colonel E.P. Roy, head of the Louisiana State Police under Governor Huey Long. Steele designed the gardens and kept them up when the house was purchased by Dr. Courtland Smith. When the house was sold again in 1995, the new buyers were delighted to discover that Steele had designed the gardens.[83]

On River Road, three miles south of Baton Rouge, the Cottage Plantation house built in 1824 was occupied from 1943 to 1945 by writer Frances Parkinson Keyes, who restored the house and employed Steele Burden. For two years, Steele worked to create a garden beneath the oaks, including in the design Cherokee roses and white wisteria. Unfortunately, the Cottage Plantation house was struck by lightning and burned down in 1960. Only ruins remain. Keyes also spent the winters in New Orleans at the Beauregard House from 1944 to her death in 1970. Because she wanted Steele's help with restoration of the walled parterre garden, she allowed him to reside in the carriage house for five years. Keyes left the house to the Beauregard-Keyes House and Garden Foundation; it is a popular tourist attraction.

Steele had lived in New Orleans and restored gardens there before. In 1938, he purchased a French Quarter house at 831–833 Dauphine Street that was originally built in 1822. He restored the building and configured it into three apartments and a personal studio. He designed the bare, neglected backyard into a large garden courtyard.[84]

Steele was also instrumental in the landscape design during the restoration of the gardens at Shadows-on-the-Teche Plantation in New Iberia in southwest Louisiana. First developed in the antebellum period, the gardens were restored in the 1950s by Weeks Hall, the last member of the original family owners. At eighty-four years old, Steele was still working with homeowners such as John Bateman, then senior vice-president of the Louisiana National Bank. Longtime friend Sue Turner said that Steele never actually had a design plan—he just walked around and said to the workers what plant to put where, and the results were always stunning.[85]

Steele had trouble finishing his gardens, though. He always felt that there was something more that should be done, and because of that Steele seldom sent invoices to the people who employed him. As late as 1993, he claimed that he never made any money from doing gardens and that when people met him around town, they would ask why he hadn't sent them a bill. Contrary to his claims, Steele did send out some invoices on printed stationery labeled "Steele Burden Landscaping, Windrush, FRD Three, Baton Rouge, LA," a few of which are found in the family archives.[86]

STORYTELLER

Mr. Steele was known in Baton Rouge as a vivid storyteller, and many of his stories have passed into the city's folklore. Steele attended LSU for a short period but did not have the demeanor to stay put in a classroom. Instead, he began to travel. He claimed to have worked his way to Europe on steamers or traveled as a stowaway.

For a few years, Steele was the keeper of a small zoo in the City Park:

> *His eyes twinkle as he tells of chasing escaped monkeys as they swung from the trees he planted. And there was the zoo's bear, Burden, who raised it from a cub, thought nothing of going into its cage to feed it, until one day,*

when it was grown, it wrapped both of its arms around his body. The bear stuck his face up to Burden's, but, rather than taking a bite out of him, it began to lick his cheeks, Burden recounts.

The true events of this story are unknown, but it was likely embellished by Steele for his listeners.[87]

Burden never took himself too seriously, as illustrated by the story of his "offices" while working for LSU. At first, he stated that he worked in part of the LSU cow barn. He moved up in recognition when a contractor finished work on the campus and left his fancy, outdoor three-staller privy, which Steele was given for his new "office." Originally, it has been located by the stadium, but Steele moved it near the maintenance barn on the edge of the campus, near Bayou Fountain. In true Burden fashion, he removed the stalls, added a little porch with wisteria growing up the posts and landscaped around it with bits of shrubbery and some sculpture, all of which made the "privy" office "one of the favorite tourist attractions of the campus at the time."[88]

The family members, too, were the subject of some of Steele's stories. In August 1950, his mother, who raised cattle at Windrush, sold a bull (known as the "Big Animal") and six of his offspring for $440 and acquired a younger bull. Steele told Ione in a letter that he felt Mama regretted selling the old bull because the new one seemed to have a "neurosis of some kind." But Steele just believed it was lack of maturity. "Then too I think Mama little realizes there does come a time in every cow's life in which they no longer have the maternal instinct and are quite content to have the stranger stay" at the other end of the pasture.[89]

Another favorite story was about the descendants of former plantation owners Steele had met. He traveled throughout Louisiana and Mississippi searching for nineteenth-century items that would eventually end up in the Rural Life Museum. Steele said that he was frugal with his limited money, and since there were no hotels, he would sleep in his truck or camp out on these collecting trips. Of course, that caused him to look, as he put it, "like a bum" when he'd turn up at farms and houses looking to buy items. But people needed money in the 1920s and 1930s, so they would sell things to him. Years later, Steele said that he'd be invited to parties at the homes of some of the people from whom he bought house items and would hear them talking about how although people were always trying to buy antiques from them, they would never sell anything because it was their "birthright." They never made the connection that Steele Burden was the bum they had sold furniture to many years earlier. He'd laugh, never say a word and go to the Rural Life Museum and sit on their chairs.[90]

Steele lived his last years in the Ollie Steele Burden Manor, and he took daily walks along the paths he created in the Windrush Gardens or went to his Rural Life Museum studio to sculpt. Until his death, he tended the plants and supervised their maintenance. He would sometimes be spotted by visitors to the museum and gardens, who would jump to the conclusion that he was a senile escapee of the nearby nursing home. He'd play along and let the do-gooders walk him back to the Burden Manor so they could enjoy the pleasure of helping an old man. The minute the "helpers" were off the grounds, Steele would walk back to his gardens and continue his work. Other times, he would be working in the plants near the Rural Life Museum's cemetery and tourists would ask where old man Burden was buried. Steele's reply: "Oh, his ashes are over there in the woods."[91]

And finally, here is one of the many myths about Baton Rouge oak trees. One day, while attending a meeting at a local garden, Steele heard someone explain the history of the live oak tree people were viewing. "It is 225 years old," the woman said. Shocked and stunned, Steele kept quiet. He had planted the tree as a sapling from the nearby woods. "I didn't tell them any better because it gave them so much pleasure to think the tree was 225 years old."[92]

MR. STEELE, THE ARTIST

Steele's crackled and glazed ceramic sculptures are collectibles throughout the world. Each was given a story and a name. "My, the end of my days still playing in mud, just a dirty old man," was his comment about the work. In the early 1940s, an LSU art professor asked Steele to try to create items from a type of Louisiana clay. From then on, Steele says, he played with clay and just pinched up the little statues. They depict Louisiana people and life, LSU football players, farmers, slaves, children playing, choirs singing and animals. Steele said that he never knew what anybody would want with them.

Steele painted and sketched as well. He believed that a person could create beautiful pictures, even when he knew nothing about art and painting techniques, if he appreciated beauty. This, Steele felt, was what he did. Painting for him was a wonderful diversion and made him more observant of human nature and more aware of the world around him. The walls of the Rural Life Museum original exhibit barn are covered with sketches of landscapes done in oils and charcoal by Steele. He drew these from images in

Steele's artwork appears throughout the museum buildings. *Courtesy of the LSU Rural Life Museum and Windrush Gardens.*

his mind and from paintings, artifacts and photographs he acquired through the years, all of which inspired him.[93]

Some of Steele's dreams were not completed in his lifetime. He had laid out a tree and shrub identification trail behind the Ione E. Burden Conference Center with the hopes to circumnavigate the entire Burden Research Center with a trail system. But after his death, Steele's plans for this were not finished nor the trails maintained. In 2000, the Burden Research Center director wanted to revive the trails. Working with volunteers from Baton Rouge Green, they began to clean the trails and restore them; they named the project Trees and Trails. Just as the trails were to be opened to the public in 2008, Hurricane Gustav hit Baton Rouge and destroyed them and the old hardwood forest at the Burden Research Center.

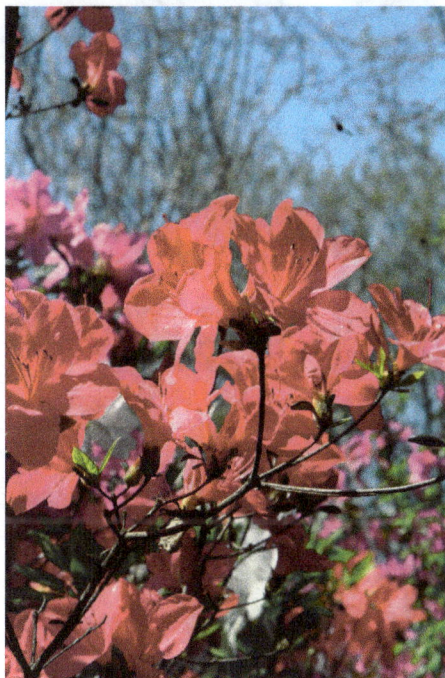

Courtesy of Jim Zietz, LSU University Relations.

"The way of cultivation
is not easy. He who
plants a garden plants
happiness." Anonymous

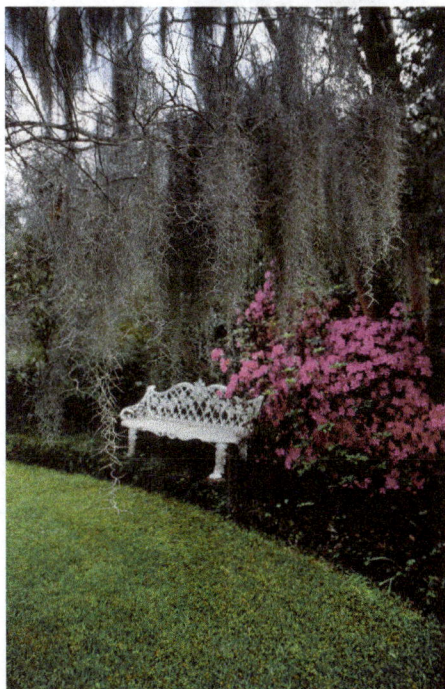

Rest awhile in the Windrush Gardens.
Courtesy of Jim Zietz, LSU University
Relations.

A walk through Windrush Gardens. *Courtesy of Jim Zietz, LSU University Relations.*

Courtesy of Jim Zietz, LSU University Relations.

Courtesy of Jim Zietz, LSU University Relations.

> "When all is said and done, is there any more wonderful sight, any moment when man's reason is nearer to some sort of contact with the nature of the world, than the sowing of seeds, the planting of cuttings, the transplanting of shrubs, or the grafting of slips." St. Augustine

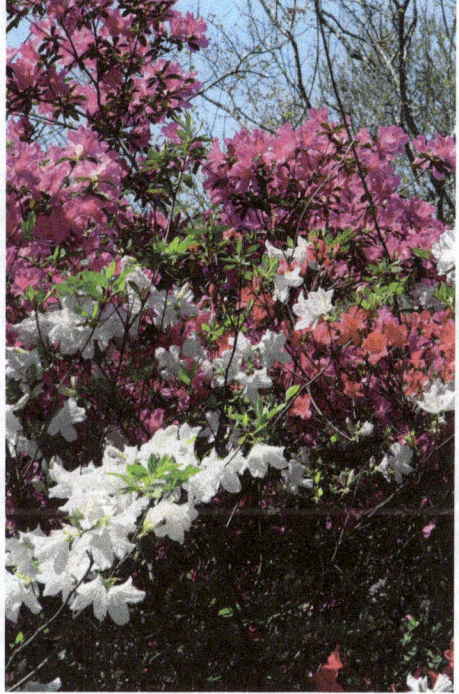

Courtesy of Jim Zietz, LSU University Relations.

Courtesy of Jim Zietz, LSU University Relations.

Courtesy of Nancy N. Colyar.

Courtesy of Jim Zietz, LSU University Relations.

"When the sun rises, I go to work. When the sun goes down I take my rest, I dig the well from which I drink, I farm the soil which yields my food, I share creation, Kings can do no more." Chinese proverb, 2500 BC

Courtesy of Jim Zietz, LSU University Relations.

Courtesy of Jim Zietz, LSU University Relations.

Courtesy of Jim Zietz, LSU University Relations.

Courtesy of Jim Zietz, LSU University Relations.

"No occupation is so delightful to me as the culture of the earth, no culture comparable to that of the garden, but though an old man, I am but a young gardener." Thomas Jefferson, *Garden Book*, 1811

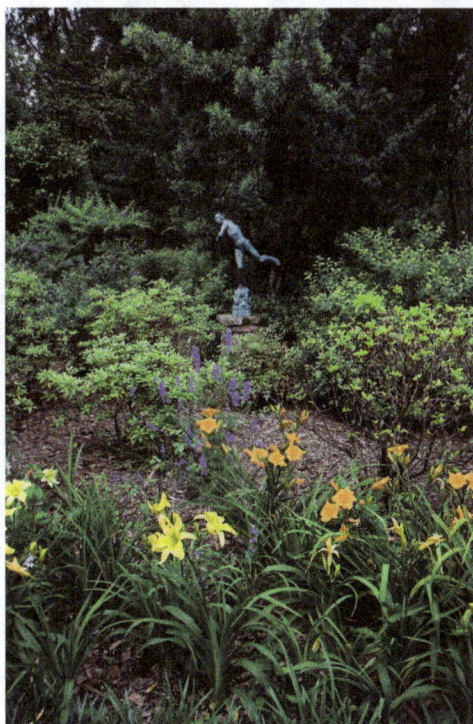

Courtesy of Jim Zietz, LSU University Relations.

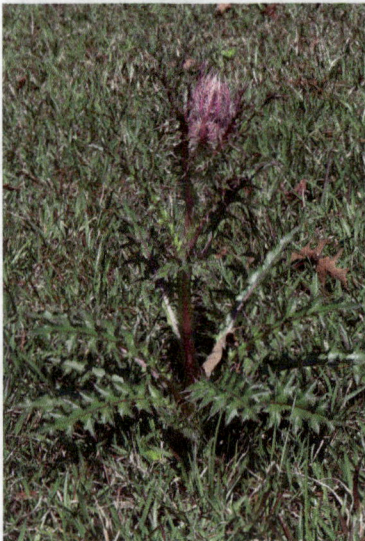

Beauty in unexpected things in the Windrush Gardens. *Courtesy of Nancy N. Colyar.*

An occasional resident of the Windrush Gardens lakes. *Courtesy of the LSU Photograph Collection, Office of Public Relations, UA, LSU Libraries.*

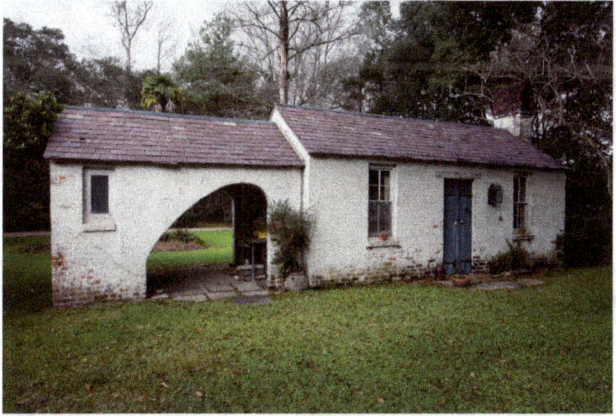

Right: Steele's garden house studio. *Courtesy of Jim Zietz, LSU University Relations.*

Below: Oak trees, a cabin and the country church await visitors. *Courtesy of the LSU Photograph Collection, Office of Public Relations, UA, LSU Libraries.*

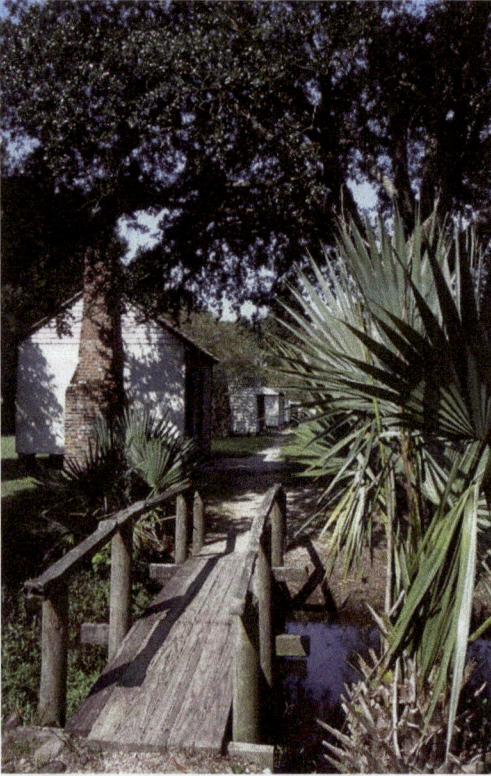

Left: People come to the Rural Life Museum and just recall the past. *Courtesy of the Rural Life Museum.*

Below: Only animal power could pull this seed planter. *Courtesy of the Rural Life Museum.*

A delightful view of the replica sugarhouse. *Courtesy of the Rural Life Museum.*

Vernacular buildings were rescued by the Rural Life Museum. *Courtesy of the Rural Life Museum.*

Buildings were taken apart and moved to the Rural Life Museum. *Courtesy of the Rural Life Museum.*

Above: Skilled and dedicated workers have restored numerous buildings. *Courtesy of the Rural Life Museum.*

Left: Every rural home required an outhouse. *Courtesy of the Rural Life Museum.*

Above: Guests visit the replica Acadian house, with its barn and beehive oven. *Courtesy of the Rural Life Museum.*

Right: A cabin porch tempts visitors to take a seat. *Courtesy of the Rural Life Museum.*

The quiet country cemetery. *Courtesy of the LSU Photograph Collection, Office of Public Relations, UA, LSU Libraries.*

A small statue of a saint in a wooden box adorns a fence. *Courtesy of the Rural Life Museum.*

Every event at the Rural Life Museum, such as harvest days, includes traditional music. *Courtesy of the Rural Life Museum.*

Steele Burden painted his views of sugar making on the plantation. *Courtesy of the Rural Life Museum.*

Exhibits include many examples of folk art, models and paintings by many Louisiana artists. *Courtesy of the Rural Life Museum.*

The Visitors' and Exhibit Center has flexible space for paintings and sculptures. *Courtesy of the Rural Life Museum.*

All his life, Steele continued to work at the museum and in the gardens. *Courtesy of Gerard Ruth.*

"Trees and Trails went from ready for ribbon cutting to ruins in hours." But many volunteers and organizations worked together with staff of the Burden Research Center to restart the project. On November 8, 2009, the trails reopened and were dedicated to the memory of Steele Burden. Two and a half miles of crushed limestone trails wind through areas of palmettos, black swamp, magnolia beech trees, American elm sycamore, cherry bark oak, yellow poplar, sweet gum, water oak, ironwood, hackberry, cypress, tupelo gum and sweet gum. Work will continue to revive "Burden's idea of a trail system to be used to educate children" through outdoor classrooms. However, others—such as Steele's idea for a Native American village beside one of the lakes—did not happen. The artifacts that he collected for the village are displayed in the Louisiana Native American section of the exhibit barn.[94]

Following Steele Burden's death, his close friends developed and had constructed the Steele Burden Memorial Orangerie to commemorate his significant contributions to Baton Rouge and Louisiana. "Part conservatory and part interpretive in construction, orangeries originally were designed to house or protect citrus trees during cold weather, hence the name." The Burden

"Your visit would be thanks enough." *Courtesy of the LSU Rural Life Museum and Windrush Gardens.*

Orangerie includes a main room for displaying tropical and subtropical plants along with four smaller rooms that hold changing displays. Designed by A. Hays Town, it opened in June 1998. Town said he had learned a great deal from his longtime friend and found Steele's use of native, maintenance-free plants in the landscape to be the perfect complement for his building designs based on historical Louisiana architecture. The orangerie is a perfect tribute to the Baton Rouge's yard man.[95]

Longtime friend and supporter of the Rural Life Museum and Windrush Gardens Ann Wilkinson said it best:

> *How fortunate we all are that Mr. Burden has donated a permanent green space, free forever from the threat of development, a place of beauty in the heart of the capital city, where we and our children can revel in natural and man-made gardens and learn from the fragments of our cultural history which he has striven to preserve. How can we thank this kind, humble and generous man for a gift so great? Simply by enjoying it. I feel sure that for "Mr. Steele," your visit would be thanks enough.[96]*

Chapter 3

LOUISIANA RURAL LIFE

The Rural Life Museum is the largest collection of material culture of nineteenth-century Louisiana, containing thousands of artifacts and thirty-two historic buildings, many of which were collected by Steele Burden. For many years, he planned a museum based on the theme of Louisiana rural and farm life. Once he, Ione and Pike decided to donate the Windrush Plantation to LSU, Steele moved forward with his plans. The first public announcement of the museum appeared in the *Sunday Advocate* on April 23, 1967. Louisiana State University was to preserve the garden areas given by the Burden family near Essen Lane in Baton Rouge. Plans included the development of a public museum depicting Louisiana rural life through items collected by Steele Burden, a five-mile walking trail around 150 acres of the woodland and man-made lakes.

Steele's collection included cooking utensils, farm implements, plantation records, sugar kettles and ox yokes. Other artifacts were a peanut wagon, steam cooking kettles, slave neck yokes, a water-propelled fan, portable sewing machines, a rudimentary typewriter and a horse-drawn hearse with a glass enclosure for the coffin once used at St. Michael's Cemetery in Convent, St. James Parish, southeast Louisiana. For the museum and gardens, Steele had also collected statues from Europe, two-hundred-year-old olive oil jars and a pre–Civil War pigeonnier. Donors such as D.H. Burleigh—the vice-president of Southdown, Inc., in 1972—gave Steele permission to move items, such as an animal-driven sugar cane crusher, from the company's property along the Mississippi River to the Rural Life Museum.

Displayed are artifacts of daily life and death, such as this wagon hearse. *Courtesy of the LSU Photograph Collection, Office of Public Relations, UA, LSU Libraries.*

Nineteenth-century cloth was woven at home. *Courtesy of the LSU Photograph Collection, Office of Public Relations, UA, LSU Libraries.*

A Living History

Steele acquired from Ambrose Storck his extensive collection of medical implements, kitchen and home furnishings, phonographs and other nineteenth-century artifacts of everyday rural life. Dr. Storck named the collection the Howell-Storck Collection in honor of his parents—natives of Toca Village in St. Bernard Parish, one parish south of New Orleans—who began the collection. These appropriate artifacts are displayed and used throughout the museum complex to help interpret Louisiana life in the rural eighteenth, nineteenth and early twentieth centuries. The original exhibit barn is itself an artifact, as its walls were Steele Burden's canvas on which he wrote, drew and painted his thoughts and images of Louisiana life. In 2010, a new visitors' and exhibit center was opened to improve the museum's ability to display and interpret the artifacts, as well as to provide more extensive educational programs to a wide variety of student and adult visitors.[97]

Based on Steele Burden's vision, there are two main areas of the Rural Life Museum in addition to the exhibit barn: the Plantation Section and the Folk Life Section, represented by vernacular architecture from Louisiana's Anglo-Saxon upland south and Gulf Coast south. The buildings in both sections are arranged to depict nineteenth-century Louisiana rural life. Within the buildings, artifacts show more details of that life. Some of the

Nineteenth-century tractors were steam powered. *Courtesy of the LSU Rural Life Museum and Windrush Gardens.*

Above: Kettles used for cooking syrup. *Courtesy of the LSU Photograph Collection, Office of Public Relations, UA, LSU Libraries.*

Left: A restored pioneer cabin. *Courtesy of the LSU Rural Life Museum and Windrush Gardens.*

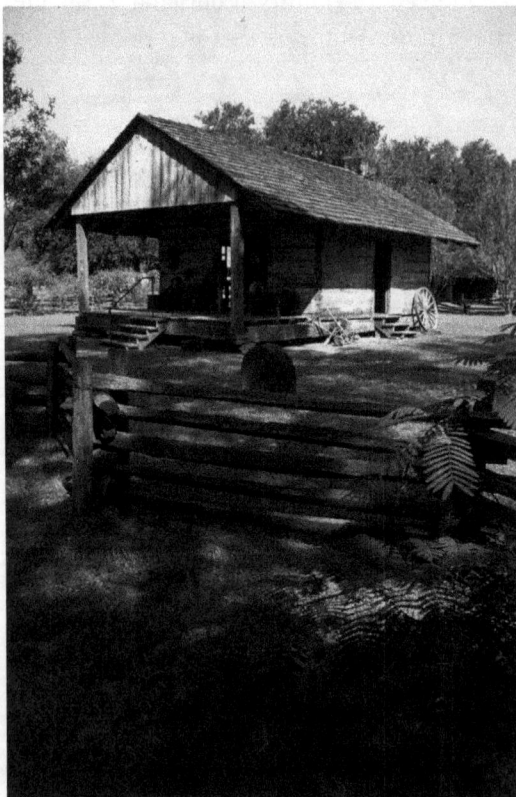

buildings included in the Plantation Section are a sugarhouse, slave cabins, an overseer's house, a sick house, a kitchen, a commissary, a schoolhouse, a blacksmith's shop and a pigeonnier. The Folk Life Section includes, among others, a country African American church, a pioneer's cabin and corncrib, a potato house, a Carolina cabin, a dogtrot house and barn, a shotgun house, a jail, Acadian cabins, a split cypress barn, a smokehouse and a post office.[98]

THE PLANTATION SECTION

The physical layout of an antebellum plantation could resemble a small village. From the river landing, the first building often was a warehouse, followed by the commissary, or plantation store. A fence defined the front of the property. The plantation house of the owners was behind the fence back from the riverbank on the next highest ground, with an oak *allée* leading from the front fence to the front steps that channeled river breezes to the house. Rainwater was collected in large cisterns near the rear of the house, and a detached kitchen stood behind those. Fire was an ever-present danger, so kitchens with open-hearth cooking were kept a safe distance away from the main house. Smokehouses, storerooms and sometimes wine cellars were also found near the kitchen. Some plantations had schoolhouses. Between the fields and slave quarters were the overseer's house and garden, blacksmith shops, stables, barns, storage sheds, other utility buildings, carriage houses, a sugar factory and a dairy. Nearby was the plantation's bell, which kept the schedule by ringing out time to work and time to rest each day. Next were the fields of crops. Louisiana plantation owners were a mixture of French colonials, Creoles and/or Anglo-Americans after 1803.[99]

Juice ground from sugar cane, a Southeast Asian tropical grass, and granulated into sugar provided Louisiana its first true economic base. Other crops did contribute to the economy along the Mississippi River, but none had the impact on the people and the economy that sugar did. Beginning in the 1750s and lasting until the Civil War, sugar produced in Louisiana made up more than 95 percent of all sugar produced in the United States. In nineteenth-century Louisiana, the plantation model that had been successful in the West Indies was adopted. The system utilized a large number of slave laborers to produce a single crop, and the rich land of the Mississippi Valley was ideal to grow indigo, tobacco, cotton and sugar. The invention of the cotton gin in 1793, which removed the cotton seed from the fiber, made cotton a much more profitable crop, especially in the higher ground

A Southeastern Asian grass, sugar cane, was the basis of the largest economy in the antebellum United States. *Courtesy of the LSU Rural Life Museum and Windrush Gardens.*

of Louisiana. Sugar cane was the most profitable crop in the lower lands below St. James Parish. Near Baton Rouge, both cotton and sugar cane were grown on the plantations.[100]

Plantation work was set by sugar cane's growing and processing requirements. During the late winter and early spring, cane was planted, stubble from the previous season was plowed, equipment was checked and repaired, the bayous were cleared as needed and river levees repaired and improved. In the early spring, the cane sprouted. Sprouts from the roots of the previous year's plants, second- or third-year plants, were known as "ratoons." These did not yield as well as plants sprouted from seed cane. Seed cane were stalks cut early before regular harvest time, to be wintered over under a thin layer of dirt. As soon as spring weather permitted, these seed cane were planted by the slaves in rows spaced six feet apart.[101]

Also in the spring, corn, the primary food for humans and animals, was planted. Both corn and sugar cane required hand-hoeing by the slaves.

Two-wheeled wagons brought the cut cane to the grinder. *Courtesy of the LSU Photograph Collection, Office of Public Relations, UA, LSU Libraries.*

Otherwise, grass and weeds would choke out the crops. Depending on the weather, corn and cane could grow tall enough to shade the ground and prevent the need for further hoeing by the Fourth of July. Mid- to late summer and early fall were the times for woodcutting. Wood was dried for a year because seasoned wood burned better under the sugar kettles. Slaves also built barrels and hogsheads to hold the processed sugar. After woodcutting, the first crop of corn was harvested and processed for humans and made into feed for the animals. Many overseers would have a second crop of corn planted at this time, to be harvested after the cane in early winter. The longer the cane was left to grow, the more sugar it yielded, but the cutting had to be timed to beat the first and sometimes early frost. In October, seed cane was cut; in November, the regular cane harvest began and ended in mid-December. Grinding and processing of the cane now became everyone's focus.[102]

Sugar cane processing involved grinding. Mules or oxen pulled open two-wheeled carts carrying the cut cane from the fields and afterward were hitched to the crusher pole that turned cast-iron grinding rollers. Slaves hand-fed the stalks into the grinder, while the animal continually circled to grind the juice from the cane. From the grinder, extracted juice flowed

Guests visit the LSU Rural Life Museum sugarhouse. *Courtesy of the LSU Photograph Collection, Office of Public Relations, UA, LSU Libraries.*

into cypress vats. By 1830, steam-powered grinders began to replace animal-powered ones until, shortly before the Civil War, most were steam-powered. The pressed stalks of cane, known as "bagasse," were discarded.[103]

Cane juice required cooking to become sugar. Slaves skimmed and cleaned debris from the juice and moved it to the sugarhouse to be boiled and crystallized. The sugarhouse, like the eighteenth-century replica at the Rural Life Museum, accomplished this through an open-kettle process. Introduced into Louisiana from the West Indies, the cooking vat arrangement of three to five kettles was sometimes called a Jamaica train, reflecting the origin of the system. Its purpose was to evaporate the water from the juice until it became thick syrup. A large brick oven had cast-iron kettles built into the top. At one end was the fire, at the other the chimney.

The largest kettle—twelve feet in diameter ("la grande") and nearest the chimney—received the juice first. In this kettle, lime was added to the juice to help remove impurities, an inexact but critical step to the process. As it boiled, scum formed from the impurities and was dipped into the scum gutters that ran along each side and the length of the evaporator. Scum was not wasted but returned to the boiling process after it settled.

At the proper time, the sugar maker ordered slaves to move the clarified juice to the next-sized kettle ("la flambeau") by use of a large wooden bucket on the end of a cantilevered pole and then into "la sirop," where the juice boiled down to a syrup. The smallest kettle, only three feet in diameter ("la batterie"), had the fire built under it for the greatest concentration of heat. Once the syrup boiled to the proper consistency required for crystallization, "striking" then occurred. This meant that the contents were removed from "la batterie" and placed into the cooling vats. A strike could happen as often as once an hour when all processes operated smoothly. This solution, "masse cuit," was emptied into wooden cooling tanks for twenty-four hours for crystallizing.

The sugar was packed into wooden hogsheads, huge barrels, which could hold 1,000 to 1,200 pounds of sugar. In order to drain off any more moisture, the hogsheads had drip holes in the base and were positioned over smaller barrels to catch the dripping molasses or sugar that didn't crystallize. Left inside in the hogsheads was pure brown sugar. Hogsheads were shipped to various markets for raw consumption, and others were shipped to several northern cities for refining into white sugar.[104]

The replica sugarhouse at the Rural Life Museum was created on-site in 1972 from drawings of original sugarhouses. For the twenty-four-hours-a-day operation for the three months of the sugar production season, October through December, a sugarhouse of this size required 7,500 cords of wood. Displayed around the sugarhouse at the Rural Life Museum are

Near the slave cabins is the horse-drawn hay cutter used by Steele Burden at LSU.
Courtesy of the LSU Rural Life Museum and Windrush Gardens.

barrels, wooden boxes and trays used for holding the raw juice, syrup and sugar and various tools used in the sugar-making process—a ladle, stirring paddle and syrup sampler. Near the sugarhouse is a cane grinder made in 1880 by the Chattanooga Plow Company and purchased in 1970 as part of the Storck Collection.

Several slave cabins at the Rural Life Museum exemplify Louisiana slave homes in use before the Civil War. Sometimes, slave cabins were made of brick, but most had wooden walls. A single pen slave cabin built circa 1840 and moved to the Rural Life Museum in 1982 from Tyron Plantation in Rapides Parish in central Louisiana was left unfinished to show the variety of construction features used. The cabin is of the typical mortise-and-tenon construction, with hand-hewn cypress sills, studs and floor joists, hewn only on the top to permit a level floor. The front exterior wall is an example of "briquette entre poteaux" (brick between posts), which would originally have been plastered over or covered with siding to protect the soft slave-made bricks from the weather. The interior of the back wall shows various stages of "bousillage," a mixture of mud and Spanish moss inserted between hand-hewn cypress studs for insulation and plastered over. Palmetto thatch or cypress shingle roofs covered the cabins. In the cabin are tools used to build the structure, such as the broadaxe that shaped the logs into beams, the foot adze that finished the top of sills and the froe that split wood into shingles.

The oldest Rural Life Museum slave cabin is a double pen, or saddlebag, construction style of about three hundred square feet total. Common to Louisiana, these cabins are one room deep and two rooms wide, with a small porch and an overhanging roof. The two rooms were divided by a central double-faced fireplace, and each room had a front door, for these double pens were occupied by two families—one in each room. One window with shutters appeared in each side wall. Occasionally, a lean-to shed was placed on the back of the cabin. Examples of farm tools such as cane knives are displayed on the front of the Rural Life Museum slave cabins, just as they would have been stored by the slaves. Inside, a rope bed, primitive hide chairs and worn cooking tools are displayed near the fireplace. The double pen slave cabin was moved from Welham Plantation.

Historian Richard Follett found many of the names of Welham Plantation slaves and identified their jobs: William Bias was the sugar maker, Jesse was the plow foreman, Southern the blacksmith, Davy the cooper (barrel maker) and Aleck Ross the carpenter.[105] The preservation of the Welham Plantation buildings at the Rural Life Museum pays homage to these men who were slaves and skilled workmen.

The overseer's house displays artifacts of plantation life. *Courtesy of the LSU Photograph Collection, Office of Public Relations, UA, LSU Libraries.*

Overseers lived in houses midway between the slave quarters and utility areas of the plantation and the owner's house. The overseer's house at the Rural Life Museum was also moved from Welham Plantation. It was occupied from the time it was built in the 1840s until 1960. The rough-hewn cypress picket fence surrounding it is typical. Fences were important to prevent animals from damaging the gardens. Also typical are the butterfly gates and the stile (steps that led up and over the fence). The one at the overseer's house is adorned with a small St. Francis of Assisi shrine, as he is the protector of animals and friend of the common man. Overseers were the supervisors of most work that occurred on the plantation.

The structure illustrates an average house of a plantation overseer. Construction of the cabin walls was made with bousillage. Future occupants added weatherboarding to the outside walls. One of the original front walls has been replaced with briquette entre poteaux. This building is typical Classical Revival style, lacking a hallway with the rooms side by side and back to back, a cedar shingle roof and a front gallery. Galleries were extensions of living and work space. One chimney served four fireplaces— two back-to-back fireplaces so that each room had its own. In the summer,

An antebellum desk from the Storck Collection is displayed in the plantation sick house. *Courtesy of the LSU Rural Life Museum and Windrush Gardens.*

attic windows were opened as part of a ventilation method, along with the French doors and the windows, to allow the maximum amount of air to circulate through the house. In the winter, the warm attic was a work place for activities such as spinning and weaving, plus storage. The overseers' houses were elevated higher than slave cabins on piers of soft slave-made brick to protect the house from flooding. The slight elevation added another ventilation effect in the summer. Consisting of a parlor (living room), dining room and bedrooms, the overseer's cabin is furnished with furniture from the nineteenth century. The rooms are overfurnished to serve as a showcase for the museum's collection of early Louisiana handmade cypress furniture. A majority of the pieces are from the Storck Collection.[106]

The health of the slaves was important to the owner as it affected their ability to work. Overseers and owners attempted to provide sufficient food to keep the slaves healthy. A diet of salt pork, cornmeal, seasonal vegetables, chickens and eggs, milk and occasional beef and seafood was common. Diseases were prevalent in Louisiana and doctors were few. Louisiana-born slaves did seem less susceptible to the yearly dreaded yellow fever, which severely affected whites. Cholera killed hundreds of whites and blacks at a time. Children also frequently died of dehydration caused by diarrhea.[107]

Within the sick house, ill slaves were cared for by the plantation mistress, the overseer or the overseer's wife, with help from female slaves. They acquired knowledge of basic medicine and treatments from experience and information shared among plantations; local newspapers or agricultural journal articles about medical remedies and with advice on caring for sick slaves as well as white families; or from medical books collected by the planter. One book, Dr. James Ewell's *The Planter's and Mariner's Medical Companion*, was sold with portions or samples of the medicines prescribed. Visits by medical doctors were rare. Some plantation owners arranged for a local doctor to make periodic visits to the plantation for a fee and room and board for a few days.

The Rural Life Plantation sick house was originally a two-room, pre–Civil War slave cabin built between 1830 and 1840 on the Welham Plantation with the same construction methods as the other slave houses. It is arranged as a plantation sick house might have appeared. One room was a treatment room and the other an infirmary for those too ill to leave or those who were contagious. On larger plantations, the sick house would have separate rooms for men and women. On smaller plantations, a sickroom might be inside the planter's house. The beds in the Rural Life Museum sick house are typical nineteenth-century rope beds with mattresses of corn shucks, Spanish moss or feathers stuffed into cotton cloth laid over ropes woven in a cross pattern for support. Beds were draped with mosquito netting when patients were present. The Woman's Auxiliary of the East Baton Rouge Parish Medical Society in 1974 gave partial funding for the restoration of the cabin displayed as the sick house and in 1975 collected medical artifacts for it.[108]

Because of the danger of fire, the plantation kitchen was set apart from the main house. Prepared food was brought from the kitchen to the main house by slaves, who also prepared food. The Rural Life Museum kitchen, built circa 1855, originally stood at Bagatelle Plantation in St. James Parish, Louisiana, and was given to the Rural Life Museum by Mr. and Mrs. Francis Henderson James. Used as a kitchen and also a schoolhouse, the briquette

Plantation kitchens were set apart because of the danger of fire. *Courtesy of the LSU Photograph Collection, Office of Public Relations, UA, LSU Libraries.*

Rural Life Museum docents demonstrate open-hearth cooking. *Courtesy of the LSU Rural Life Museum and Windrush Gardens.*

entre poteaux structure was constructed of plantation-made bricks, soft and poorly made, and covered with wood siding that kept the bricks from deteriorating. As is typical of nineteenth-century kitchens, a pivoting metal crane suspends iron pots over a wood fire in the large, open fireplace. Many of the kitchen items displayed were used by their owners through the early twentieth century, such as the oyster roaster, biscuit roller, sugar wafer irons and spaghetti maker. Mortars and pestles—or, in South Louisiana French, pilons and piles—were used, depending on their size, for hulling rice or corn, crushing spices or grinding sassafras leaves into filé. Filé was one of many spices and cooking ingredients brought to Louisiana by African slaves and has been used extensively in Louisiana cooking for generations.

A plantation kitchen would have its own garden for growing seasoning and medicinal herbs, fresh vegetables, fruits and flowers. Corn, potatoes and other crops grown in the fields also supplemented the kitchen gardens' produce. Cooks under the supervision of the plantation owner's wife maintained the kitchen gardens. Surrounded by a fence to keep out animals such as deer, the focal point of the Rural Life Museum kitchen garden is a sundial in the center of a round growing bed. Birdhouses made of gourds

Commissaries, like general stores, became country gathering places. *Courtesy of the LSU Photograph Collection, School of Architecture, UA, LSU Libraries.*

The interior counter of the commissary is original to the building. *Courtesy of the LSU Photograph Collection, School of Architecture, UA, LSU Libraries.*

A cash register from the Gianelioni plantation commissary. *Courtesy of the LSU Photograph Collection, School of Architecture, UA, LSU Libraries.*

are hung around the kitchen garden. The birdhouses were used to attract helpful birds such as purple martins that ate mosquitoes and mockingbirds that chased away scavengers such as crows.

After the Civil War, the plantation commissaries developed to supply sharecroppers or tenant farmers, who were ex-slaves or former landowners, with goods and food for a price. The commissary building at the Rural Life Museum originated as a storeroom on the Welham Plantation circa 1830–35 and became a commissary in 1880. When it was moved to the Rural Life Museum in 1972, a back wall and porch were added. Original to the building is a marble counter containing bins for storing grains and other foods. Commissaries were essentially general stores that stocked food, farm tools and other hardware, cloth and threads, tobacco and candy. One part of the store was always a social gathering place where men played card games or families stopped to visit. Yeomen farmers also bartered their crops with the commissary for items they could not produce themselves, such as coffee, flour, cloth and tools.[109]

Schoolhouses on plantations were attended by the children of white workers such as the overseers, managers, assistant overseers and those from nearby plantations. Sometimes children of nearby yeomen farmers might attend. Planters' children frequently had tutors or were sent away to boarding schools. Tutors hired by plantation owners were given room and board, a salary, an assigned slave as a personal helper, the use of a horse and a vacation. Many times, the tutors were hired from northern schools and expected to teach classics, Latin and Greek, to the youngest children. The less wealthy planters sometimes banded together to hire a teacher for groups of children, known as a subscription school. A separate building might be designated as a schoolhouse, or classes could take place in one planter's home. Slaves were seldom taught to read or write.

The schoolhouse building at the Rural Life Museum was built about 1835 on Welham Plantation as a two-room addition with a central chimney to the overseer's house, and both were moved in 1971. Although originally intended to be a kitchen, it was in use as a schoolhouse until about 1930. The addition was connected by a raised walkway at a right angle to the rear of the overseer's house. After it was moved to Rural Life Museum, the unit was detached from the overseer's house and converted to a one-room schoolhouse for the museum to display items used by nineteenth-century children for school and other activities. None of the items in the schoolhouse is original to it.

Adapted in 1971 from a 1840s double pen slave cabin moved from Welham Plantation, the blacksmith's shop at the Rural Life Museum is also

Blacksmiths repaired and built tools and shoed the animals. *Courtesy of the LSU Photograph Collection, Office of Public Relations, UA, LSU Libraries.*

of mortise-and-tenon construction. After the cabin was moved, the walls were reconstructed with brick. The original flooring was removed and replaced with brick for a fireproof floor. A forge for heating the metal and a sharpening stone are requirements of the blacksmith shop. A free-standing chimney with a twelve-inch-deep firebox serves the forge. The hole in the bottom center accommodates the bellows or blower. The hearth brickwork extends to form a flat table, where newly finished pieces were placed to cool or to hold pieces of iron to be forged. A firmly anchored anvil and a rack of tools are within easy reach. The forge in the Rural Life Museum blacksmith's shop is a working replica of one that formerly existed at New Hope Plantation in St. James Parish and is used in demonstrations by local blacksmiths.[110] Resident blacksmiths were the creators and repairers of all ironwork on the plantation. Most farming tools were made of iron, as were horseshoes, cooking equipment, gates, harness connectors and wagon wheels. Iron crosses were made for graves. Slaves were sometimes trained to be blacksmiths.

Pigeons and their eggs were food for early Louisianans. The birds were kept in small buildings raised one story above the ground to improve air circulation, protect the birds from predators and encourage them to roost.

Pigeons also provided fertilizer for the garden. Also called dovecotes, as doves were housed in the same type of buildings, they were sometimes decorative, matching the main house's architectural details. The Rural Life Museum pigeonnier was built by Joseph Curry in 1892 when he moved to Mound Place Plantation in Tensas Parish, two miles from St. Joseph, northeast Louisiana, and was donated in 2003 by Patricia Curry Bagwell, the third generation of the Curry family to own Mound Place.

Bells on plantations were used for multiple purposes: calling workers to the fields, to lunch and to home at the end of the day. They were also rung during celebrations; for alerts of danger, such as fires and crevasses in Mississippi River levees; and to announce the arrival of guests and steamboats. The oldest bell at the Rural Life Museum—dated 1791, from Manchac Plantation, near Sunshine in Iberville Parish, mid-south Louisiana—was probably cast in France or Spain. With an ornate cross cast in relief on the side, it was originally intended for church use. The exhibit barn houses most of the museum's bell collection, containing bells cast in northern foundries and floated downriver to plantations in Louisiana from the 1830s through the 1850s. Bonne Esperance Plantation, St. James Parish and Cinclaire Plantation, near Port Allen in West Baton Rouge Parish, received bells this way, and those are now in the Rural Life Museum. One later bell is from the Standard Oil Company's steel towboat *Amos K. Gordon*, christened in 1933. Mounted on a brick column, shorter than its original thirty-foot one, is the bell from a plantation owned by Valcour Aime near Vacherie, also in St. James Parish. The plantation bell mounted near the overseer's house is from Monroe Plantation near Union in St. James Parish and is marked "G.W. Coffin & Co., Buckeye Bell Foundry, Cincinnati," Ohio. The wrought-iron yoke and straps on the bell are original.

THE FOLK LIFE SECTION

The Rural Life Museum Folk Life Section buildings reflect the ethnic culture and character of their various Louisiana builders. A variety of people settled in antebellum Louisiana. Yeomen farmers established homes in north Louisiana and the eastern piney woods; Acadian hunters and fishermen founded settlements in southwest Louisiana; and other ethnic immigrants homesteaded throughout the state. Folk (or vernacular) architecture is defined as "structures built by and for the people who occupied them or by those of the same cultural standing." These builders copied what families

Above: Vernacular buildings were dismantled, moved and reassembled at the museum.
Courtesy of the LSU Photograph Collection, Office of Public Relations, UA, LSU Libraries.

Left: The 1870s church was continuously used for worship services through the late 1960s.
Courtesy of Darelyn Marshall, the LSU Rural Life Museum and Windrush Gardens.

and neighbors had built before them based on tradition and custom. Building types, "like heirlooms, were passed on from generation to generation, with little change. The divergent construction traits illustrate the various cultures of Louisiana settlers." The section includes a country African American church, a pioneer's cabin and corncrib, a Carolina cabin, a dogtrot house and barn, a shotgun house, a jail, Acadian cabins and a split cypress barn, among others.[111]

During Reconstruction after the Civil War, African Americans in Louisiana formed their own churches, such as the one now at the Rural Life Museum. African American communities developed around these churches, where the members had religious independence. The small country African American Church stood at College Point, St. James Parish, south of Baton Rouge and west of New Orleans, near Welham Plantation from the time it was built in the 1870s until it was moved to the Rural Life Museum in 1973. Many congregations worshiped in the church, and the last was the College Grove Baptist Association from 1893 until the late 1960s.

Residents of College Point who attended services in the church were workers at Welham Plantation, and some were descendants of slaves. Descendants of the congregation still visit the church at the Rural Life Museum. Reverend

The interior of the African American church. *Courtesy of the LSU Photograph Collection, Office of Public Relations, UA, LSU Libraries.*

Near the church stands a 1926 statue by sculptor Hans Schuler. *Courtesy of the LSU Photograph Collection, Office of Public Relations, UA, LSU Libraries.*

John H. Johnson and congregation spokesman James Grayol feared that the church building would slowly fall into ruin once the congregation no longer met there. To ensure the church building's preservation, they donated it to the Rural Life Museum. The church was built in the Gothic Revival style, representing country Gothic, with a central aisle that ends in a three-sided apse, with modified lancet windows and side doors. The pews and altar are original to the church. It is very basic, with little adornment other than the painted glass windows that gave the look of a more expensive stained glass. The church is used as a display room for religious artifacts from different faiths.[112]

Near the church stands a statue that depicts an elderly African American man tipping his hat, sculpted by Hans Schuler in 1926, an American artist of

A Living History

German descent and director of the Maryland Institute of Art. The statue was commissioned by Jackson L. Bryan, a prominent white businessman in Natchitoches, Louisiana, and the son of a slave owner. Bryan stated that he wished the statue to convey his gratitude and friendship to Louisiana's African Americans and their importance in Louisiana's agricultural development. For many years, it stood in the town square of Natchitoches, northwest Louisiana, until the 1960s, when local African Americans pointed out the negative impact and impression the statute created. In 1975, Bryan's daughter donated it to the Rural Life Museum. Steele Burden had it placed

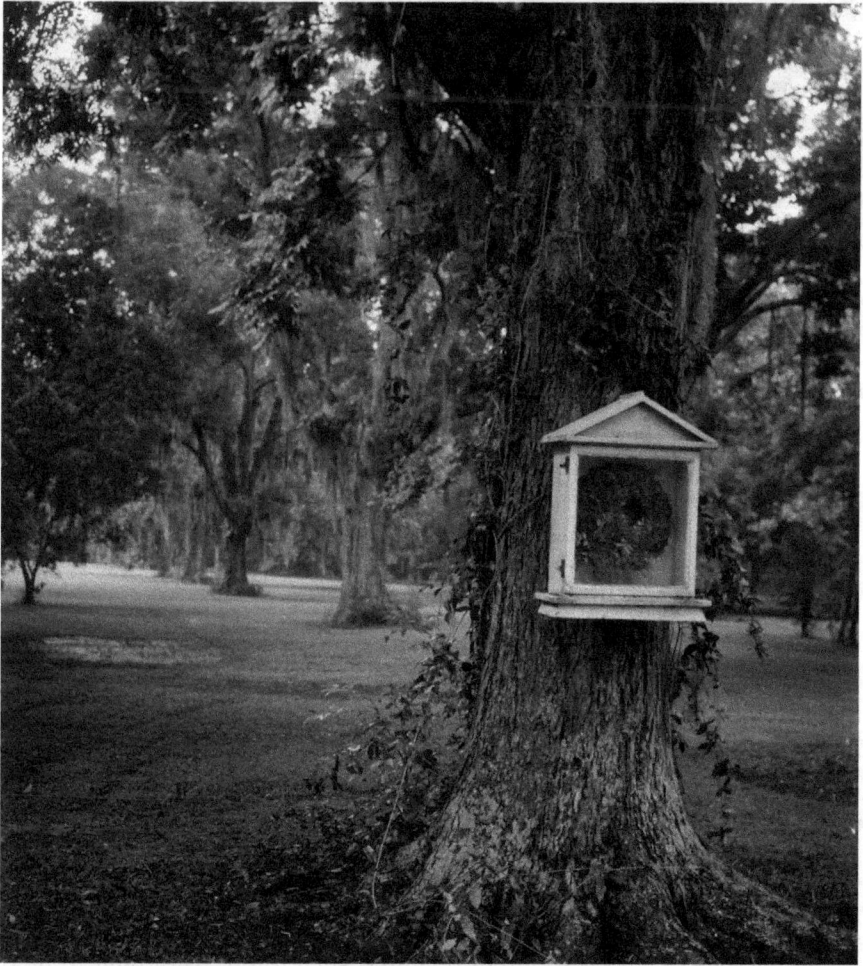

Immortelles, glass-fronted wooden boxes, contained wreaths of the deceased's hair, glass, wire or immortelle flowers. *Courtesy of the LSU Rural Life Museum and Windrush Gardens.*

The cemetery contains examples of crosses from many cultures. *Courtesy of the LSU Photograph Collection, Office of Public Relations, UA, LSU Libraries.*

outside the gate of the museum, and it was the first artifact that visitors saw. Out of context with the era in which it was created, and with no interpretive information, the statue's meaning and placement was unclear. Therefore, in 2010 it was moved near to the African American church.[113]

Until 1983, when Ione Burden was interred there, the Rural Life Museum church cemetery was a simulated one, created to show a rural country church graveyard typical in Louisiana. It contains grave markers from the entire state. Elaborate wrought-iron crosses show the work of skilled blacksmiths of the nineteenth century; plainer crosses reflect Anglo-Saxon ancestry; decorative crosses signify Spanish culture; and the fleur-de-lis design, French.

Near some graves are immortelles, small wooden boxlike structures mounted on posts or trees. Originally they would have contained a wreath woven of hair from the deceased or from glass beads or threads, kept as a permanent memorial. The graveyard contains a tomb constructed at the Rural Life Museum to show the above-ground burial used throughout south Louisiana, where land is prone to flooding. Such tombs were built to hold several generations of family members, the most recently deceased in caskets

Steele Burden overseeing the restoration of a vernacular building. *Courtesy of the LSU Rural Life Museum and Windrush Gardens.*

and the others, interred below. Poorer people who could not afford tombs were buried in the ground despite the danger of floods.[114]

Many iron crosses, the cast-iron and sheet metal entrance gate and the shrouded urn are from St. Michael's Cemetery in Convent, Louisiana. The obelisk in the cemetery marked the graves of brothers Henry and Albert O'Neal, originally interred in the Jones Creek Baptist Church Cemetery after they were killed in an infamous shootout. In 1895, the church served a prosperous farming community near Harrell's Ferry Road and the Amite River in East Baton Rouge Parish. By the 1970s, when the obelisk was moved to the Rural Life Museum for preservation, the small Jones Creek Baptist Church Cemetery had fallen into decay.[115]

As the United States expanded, many yeomen farmers migrated to Louisiana. They were, and continued to be, subsistence farmers, with all family members, including the children, working to grow enough food to feed themselves and the farm animals. Yeomen farmers, primarily of Scotch-Irish descent from the Carolinas, arrived in the great 1800s westward movement to the South and lived in such cabins. Fertile land near rivers and major bayous was owned by large plantations, so yeomen settled in the less fertile piney woods and hills. They chopped down trees, cleared the land and developed small farms, typically less than one hundred acres in size— eking out an existence in what has been called a "hog and corn economy." Animals such as hogs, cattle, sheep, goats and chickens provided wool, eggs, milk, butter and meat. Cotton, when it was grown, was sold to stores for things the farmer could not produce, such as farm tools, sugar and other food, cloth, medicine and oil.[116]

An abundance of tall, straight, virgin pine trees in east and north Louisiana were harvested by settlers for building cabins and farm buildings. Nineteenth-century pine buildings have survived in good condition because lumber from

A pioneer cabin in its original location. *Courtesy of the LSU Rural Life Museum and Windrush Gardens.*

Sugar kettles are displayed throughout the museum grounds. *Courtesy of the LSU Rural Life Museum and Windrush Gardens.*

the rosin-saturated heart of pine trees was resistant to insects and decay. Built about 1810, the pioneer cabin at the Rural Life Museum was lived in by five generations of one family until 1960. The cabin and a corncrib were moved from Sunny Hill, Washington Parish, east Louisiana, in 1972, when they were donated by the heirs of Mary Richardson Carter (1868–1955). It is a single pen cabin of heart pine logs planed smooth and pegged together, placed on supports of native rock (hematite), with a chimney made of woven wooden lattice of thin branches (known as wattle or cats) and mortar made of mud mixed with straw, sand, clay and dung (known as daub). It has a center ridgepole, hand-hewn support beams, milled logs with square notch construction and heart pine floors. The interior walls were whitewashed, and the lofts were added after the cabin was reassembled at the Rural Life Museum. A cypress bed from a Tangipahoa Parish (also east Louisiana) log cabin with a corn shuck mattress and mosquito bars and nets is typical of the era.

Built in 1880, the corncrib's function was to store the very important corn crop year round. Corn does not reseed itself, so seed corn was set aside each year and kept dry and protected in the corncrib or by hanging it from the rafters in a spilt cypress barn. The corncrib sits on supports of native rock to raise it two feet off the ground for air passage to dry the corn, and it is made of saddle notched, heart pine logs.[117]

Corn shucks were in abundance and used for bedding, floor coverings, chair seats and brooms and made into toys along with the cobs. Cobs were also fed to the hogs and used for torches, bottle stoppers and even toilet paper. Every part of the corn was used for the family's needs. Corn was commonly used in place of money. When the farmer's corn was milled, he paid the miller with part of his corn. When the tenant farmer's rent was due, he paid with a portion of the crop. "It was legally recognized as tender in commercial transactions throughout early America."[118]

Potatoes were another important crop for pioneers. Built in 1850, the potato house is a single pen outbuilding of hand-hewn cypress with half-dovetail joints and hand-split cypress roof shingles. Mud daubing is used between the cracks. Originally, it was located in Livonia, Louisiana, and donated to the Rural Life Museum by Mr. and Mrs. Ralph Olinde.

Another example of a Carolina cabin is from the eastern Louisiana Florida Parishes. A one-and-a-half-story pine log cabin that once stood on cypress piers has dovetail notches in hand-hewn logs, a single-gable room, a front and back porch and an interior constructed of hand-hewn pine. The sleeping loft was reached by interior narrow steps resembling a ladder. The front and back doors are original board-and-batten pine doors with wrought-iron hinges. The cabin's chimney is a reproduction of the original wattle-and-daub chimney.

Owned by the Stoner-Athens family from the 1870s until donated to the Rural Life Museum in 2000, this cabin was located on Greenwell Springs Road (known first as the Baton Rouge–Greensburg Road) along the Amite River at Stoney Point in East Baton Rouge Parish. It was probably constructed between 1830 and 1850. Reverend Abraham Stoner, originally from Ohio, purchased the cabin and land in 1871 and grew cotton. The cabin was also used as a way station on the stagecoach route from Greensburg to Baton Rouge, according to Stoner family lore. The stagecoach stopped to change horses, and the passengers ate and drank at the Stoner cabin. The road was well traveled because one of the five Louisiana U.S. Land Offices where settlers were required to file land claims was located in Greensburg.

Julia Harriet (Hattie) Stoner Athens was born in the cabin on August 26, 1876. Hattie lived almost 101 years, most of them in her cabin. She is buried at the Stoner family cemetery near Stoney Point. A mahogany pianoforte was the only original Stoner cabin furniture remaining when the house was moved to the Rural Life Museum. Her grandchildren, Julia Athens Read, James E. Athens, Robert S. Athens and William L. Athens, inherited the property and donated the cabin to the Rural Life Museum. Hibernia National Bank donated funds for the relocation and restoration of the Stoner-Athens Cabin. W.J. Brown and the Rural Life Museum staff dismantled and restored the cabin.

A dogtrot house consists of two rooms of equal size divided by a central breezeway half as wide as a room. Front and rear porches (or galleries) were half the width of the rooms. This was the most common house type in Louisiana before 1930 and is a symbol of the upland south culture of north Louisiana. Nicknamed "dogtrot" because dogs often slept on the breezeway, such cabins in other locations had different names, such as "pen and passage" and, in northern Alabama, "possum trot." Wattle (cat) and daub chimneys are on the exterior of each end. Windows on either side of the kitchen fireplace were added later than the original construction. The house was constructed of pine hand-hewn beams and logs with square notch corners and cedar-shake shingles. Some features that were added after the house was moved to the Rural Life Museum included window sashes and doors to an attic area in the breezeway.

Curator John Dutton searched for an authentic example of a dogtrot house for the Rural Life Museum for many years and found this one thirty-five miles west of Alexandria, Rapides Parish, in central Louisiana. Partially constructed in the 1860s it was completed in the 1870s when acquired by Thomas Neal Sr., of whom little is known. His descendants lived in the house until 1976, and a portrait of Mr. Neal's son survives on display over the cabin's mantel. Private donors aided with the cost of the move of the house to the Rural Life Museum and the cost of restoration in 1979.[119]

The original site of the dogtrot house was in an area in which people (referred to locally as Redbones) made their homes. Interracial marriages among blacks, whites and Native Americans were common in the area that today includes parts of Rapides, Allen and Vernon Parishes in the middle and west of Louisiana. The first Europeans in the area were Spanish and

French. Culture, architecture and lifestyles of the upland south came to the area with settlers from Virginia, Maryland and the Carolinas.

From the early 1800s and through the Civil War, this remote, heavily forested buffer zone between Texas and Louisiana, served as a "no man's land" for outlaws and fugitives, first as a Spanish territory and then as a state. Families and outlaws settled their own disputes without benefit of lawmen. Family lore states that the bullet holes on the right wall of the front porch of the cabin behind the shutter happened when a stranger shot and killed one of the sons. The other family members killed the man but could not identify him, and the story ends there. These bullet holes are the only physical signs of violence on a Rural Life Museum building.

Dogtrot houses usually had dogtrot barns behind or to the side of the house, built of the same materials as the house. The Stoker log barn is a dogtrot-like structure with a double pen and an open passage between pens. The barn was constructed of hand-hewn pine logs with a single-gable roof covering the storage cribs, a central passageway with an arched roof and galleries. The wooden hinges, the log troughs, harness pegs and floor of the right crib are original to the barn. The original roof was replaced by the family in 1929, and the current cedar-shake roof was installed at the museum. Hay was stored in one crib, and corn and grain were in the other. Mules and horses were stabled in the seven stalls.

In 1818, the Stokers settled near Bayou Honda, a small creek about a mile northeast of where Fort Jessup, Sabine Parish, upper-midwest Louisiana, would be established in 1824. The Stokers were immigrants typical of the nineteenth century from Scotland, who pushed south and west with groups of relatives and/or neighbors. From Native American and Spanish settlers, the Stoker family acquired substantial land and, unlike most other settlers to the area, became wealthy slave owners. Used by the Stoker family for over 150 years, the barn was originally built about 1845–48. It was also used as a stagecoach stop for those traveling from Natchitoches, Louisiana, to Many, Louisiana, on the El Camino Real (the King's Highway). This well-known landmark and Mrs. Stoker are described in noted Boston landscape architect Frederick Law Olmsted's book *A Journey through Texas, or a Saddle Trip on the Southwestern Frontier, 1822–1827*.

James Stoker, Rebecca Stoker Kyle and their father, Riley J. Stoker, donated the barn to the Rural Life Museum in 1999 in honor of R.J. and Bernice Stoker. The barn was dismantled by restoration contractor W.J. Brown and museum staff and reassembled at the museum. Tom Phillips, longtime member of the Friends of the Rural Life Museum and a friend of the Stoker family, facilitated the donation. Mrs. Paula G. Manship donated funding for the relocation and restoration of the Stoker Barn.

Familiar throughout Louisiana, shotgun houses offer maximum interior space with minimal use of materials and were popular as tenant farmer and sharecropper houses, plantation or company farm offices and cheap city dwellings. Shotgun houses are long and narrow, made of lumber with board-and-batten, raised on short piers and usually three rooms deep and one room wide, with a door at each end and a front-gabled hip roof overhanging a small front porch. The shotgun style of vernacular architecture was brought to New Orleans circa 1800 by immigrants from Haiti. "The name 'shotgun' derives from the straight-line arrangement of the rooms and doors; supposedly, a shot fired through the front door would pass out the back door without hitting a wall."[120]

Interpreted as a late nineteenth-century plantation office, the shotgun house at the Rural Life Museum was constructed circa 1877–80 for a dwelling on Augusta Plantation in the Bayou Goula area of Iberville Parish, near West Baton Rouge Parish, and donated by Denis Murrell in 1976. The back room with the side porch is original to the house, but an interior wall and fireplaces were removed to create space. Office items from the nineteenth century are displayed as part of the interpretation, including a table from the Sumter House Saloon that stood on Third Street in downtown Baton Rouge and a desk made about 1900 for LSU president Thomas Boyd by cadets.

Formerly located at Oak Ridge in Morehouse Parish, northeast Louisiana, the jail structure is believed to be the only surviving pre–Civil War wooden jail in Louisiana, although many brick jails of the period are still in existence. The circa 1835–60 building was protected from decay or destruction because a barn was built that completely enclosed it in the early 1900s by the Davis family, who inherited the property. State senator Robert Barham grew up near the original location of the jail. Due to concern for the preservation of the jail and his interest in the Rural Life Museum, Barham encouraged Emily McEnery Murphy and the McEnery family to donate the jail. It was dismantled and reassembled at the Rural Life Museum in 2002.

The jail building of twelve feet by twenty-two feet was divided into two rooms with small windows. There is a single entrance door and one door between rooms. The walls, floors and ceiling are built of three sets of heart pine boards laminated together with thousands of nails spaced no more than two inches apart. Each set was made by laying boards next to each other and nailing planks diagonally across them and then flipping them over and nailing a second diagonal layer. These could not be penetrated with an axe

Steele Burden's drawing of an Acadian cabin. *Courtesy of the Burden Family Papers, LLMVC, LSU Libraries.*

or hatchet. The jail has no corner posts or framing material. Originally, the gable roof was probably covered with wooden shingles before being replaced by tin. Chains and shackles are located on the walls of the cells, as they might have been when it was used as a jail.

Creole style, or Louisiana colonial, is defined as locally adapted architecture combined with elements from many traditions. A West Indies model distinguished by an open porch on three sides is the form that arrived in Louisiana with French planters. In Louisiana, it was further adapted to contain an English-style internal chimney, a French wraparound mantel, an umbrella roof from Canada and braced timber framing like that used in Normandy. Three types of Creole houses evolved: a single-story cottage, a raised two-story plantation house and a townhouse. Louisiana Acadian style evolved from the small Creole cottage.

The earliest-built Acadian cabins were simple ones on piers of cypress blocks or bricks. Only two rooms existed, a parlor and one narrow bedroom, with no internal hallways, but each had a window and door from the gallery. The design permitted good ventilation. Gabled roofs, covered by cypress shingles, overhung the porch supported by cypress postlike columns. Bousillage filled cypress timber walls, which might eventually be plastered. A steep, narrow stairway led from the front porch to the attic

Acadians settled in southwestern Louisiana, where they adapted the Creole cottage design for their homes. *Courtesy of the LSU Rural Life Museum and Windrush Gardens.*

space, used as a sleeping loft. In the French style, chimneys were located on end walls and not inside, as was the English style. Open-beam wood ceilings were most common.

Acadians were descendants of French Catholic settlers to Nova Scotia in the sixteenth and seventeenth centuries. When Great Britain gained the area after war with France, the Acadians were forced to renounce Catholicism or leave Nova Scotia. Many of the displaced Acadians found their way to Louisiana in 1765 by way of St. Domingo and settled in the southwestern prairie of the Attakapas district, west of the Mississippi River and above New Orleans around St. Martinsville and Opelousas. In Louisiana, they found a Spanish, not French, government in control. However, the Catholic Spanish welcomed the immigrants. The Acadians formed a close-knit society and became farmers, fishermen and trappers on the abundant land. Others established cattle ranches.[121]

One of the many uses of fences was for drying clothes. *Courtesy of the LSU Rural Life Museum and Windrush Gardens.*

A Living History

One of the oldest surviving Acadian dwellings in Louisiana was moved to the Rural Life Museum in 2005. Built between 1800 and 1815, the house and property on the east bank of Bayou Lafourche three miles from Labadieville, lower south Louisiana, was acquired by Jean Charles Germain Bergeron. In 1899, Henry Pitre purchased the house but allowed the former owner to remain in the house until her death. She died in 1906, whereupon Henry and Lea Ayo Pitre and their five children moved to the farm and into the house. Their descendants lived in the house until 1970.

In 1909, Henry Pitre expanded the small house with two more rooms, a parlor and bedroom and divided the original living room into two bedrooms. He replaced the original wattle-and-daub chimney with a smaller brick one. A Norman truss roof (common to French Nova Scotia)—steeply pitched and supported by a horizontal room timber on heavy inner truss blades and vertical posts—was replaced with a gabled roof after 1835. Original bousillage entre poteaux construction remains in the front wall. Sometime between 1920, when Henry Pitre died, and 1950, the rear parlor/bedroom ell was removed and used as a small country store on the same property. The Jean Charles Germain Bergeron House was donated to the Rural Life Museum by Mr. and Mrs. Jack Wise of Thibodeaux, Louisiana. Its restoration was supported by the Friends of the Rural Life Museum, and the museum docents supported the costs of furnishing the house.

Split-cypress barns were built and used by Acadians. The Rural Life Museum split-cypress barn was constructed about 1870 in the Part Barré area of St. Landry Parish, central Louisiana, and then moved to the Orange Grove Store in Point Coupee Parish, one parish east of the original location. It was acquired in 2002 from the Orange Grove Store and moved to the museum. Split-cypress barns called pieux barns represent the type of barn thrown up quickly and inexpensively in remote rural areas. Because of its cheap and hurried construction with whatever materials were near at hand, this one is a unique survivor of the nineteenth century, most likely because it is built of cypress native to south Louisiana, whose lumber lasted many years. Such barns were used by yeomen farmers, hunters, trappers and fishermen to stable animals and to store corn to feed them. The single crib barn with a shed on each side was raised off the ground for ventilation and to protect the corn from vermin and rot. The right-side shed of this barn was originally used as a blacksmith shop, and evidence of this can still be seen.

Also displayed at the Rural Life Museum is a replica of an Acadian house constructed in 1975 on-site, of traditional mortise-and-tenon construction and half-timber framing filled with bousillage. The interior walls were completed using new lumber and sheetrock plastered to give the appearance of a bousillage finish. The roof is sawn pine shingles. The house was designed and constructed with similar components and techniques employed by Acadian builders in the prairies of southwest Louisiana. The cypress lumber used in the main framing and woodwork of the house was originally part of a mule barn dismantled at Rapidan Plantation on the east bank of the Mississippi River in St. James Parish, south Louisiana. The reproduction house is used in conjunction with the Bergeron House by museum docents to interpret Acadian lifestyles.

Based on a design common to south Louisiana Acadians, a copy of a large beehive oven was constructed in 1997 near the replica Acadian house. After a fire burned to ashes within the oven, the ashes were raked out from the base with a wooden rake, and cornmeal or dough was placed directly on the base. The heat held in the oven walls cooked the food. The only way to adjust temperature was to close the door. Experience in using the oven taught the cook when food was done.

In order to demonstrate farm activities, some structures not original to the nineteenth century have been adapted. The building used as the smokehouse was built in the early 1930s as a train depot and moved to the Rural Life Museum in 1973. Smoking meat was a method used on plantations and small farms to preserve pork, beef and wild game. Smoked meat would keep without spoiling until needed.

The Rural Life Museum post office, built in 1897, was originally named the Colomb Post Office and was located at the previous site of Webre Plantation, in St. James Parish, southeast Louisiana. The Colomb service was discontinued in 1915. Two years later, the building was not moved from its original spot, but rather its name was changed to the Romeville Post Office, as the village had become known as Romeville, and mail service resumed. The Rome family and the Webre family had intermarried, and the majority of the five hundred people in the village had the surname Rome. The one-room, gable-roofed cypress building measures six feet by four feet three inches and stands on raised wooden piers. Original cypress board-and-batten doors and window shutters remain, as well as the original linoleum floor and wall shelf. Contained inside are the original mail scale, some postal stamps and a U.S. Postal Book from the period.

The United States Postal Service began a consolidation of rural post offices in 1955, and by 1960 the Romeville Post Office was discontinued. Of course, by that time rural route delivery was available. The Colomb/Romeville Post Office building was donated to the Rural Life Museum in

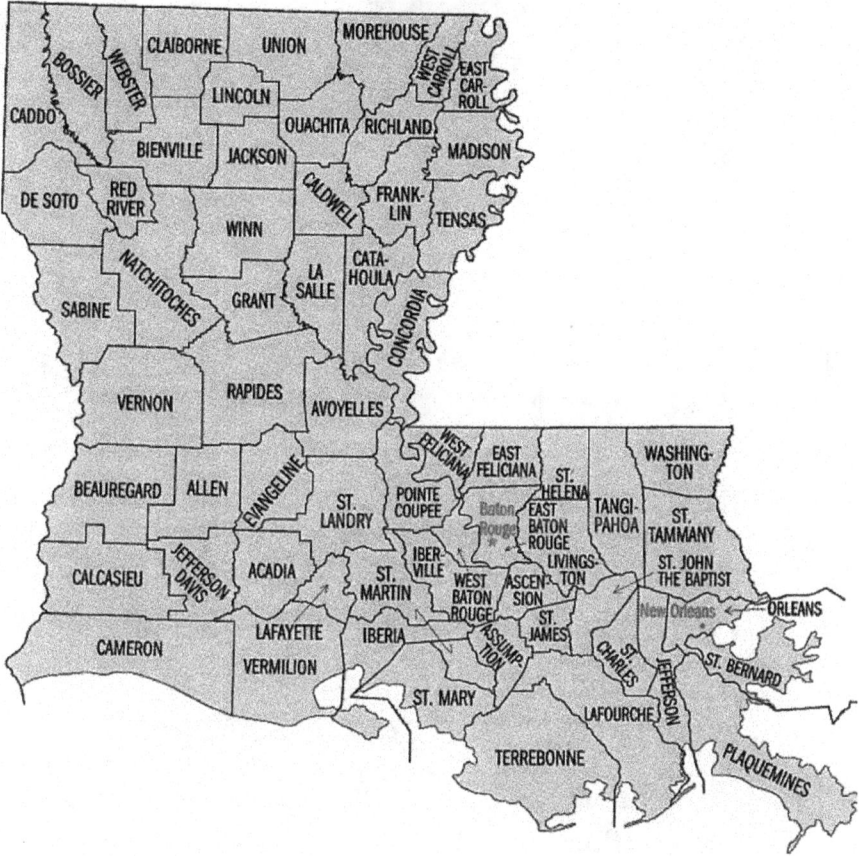

In Louisiana, counties are called parishes, as this map shows. *Courtesy of U.S. Census Quick Facts.*

2002 by Dr. and Mrs. Robert Judice and Robert Judice Jr. It was moved and restored by museum staff.

The Rural Life Museum exhibit barn, the Plantation Section and the Folk Life Section buildings exemplify through artifacts and vernacular architecture life in rural Louisiana from the late eighteenth to the early twentieth centuries. Preservation of buildings and artifacts and interpretation of, and education about, Louisiana's people, places, architecture, gardens, rural life and economy are the missions of the LSU Rural Life Museum. Combined with the mission for the Windrush House and Gardens to provide a space where visitors may appreciate a simple life and the beauty of nature, the future of both is assured through the continued efforts of the community.

Chapter 4

"TO PRESERVE THE
RURAL SETTING"

On January 15, 2010, the LSU Rural Life Museum and Windrush Gardens opened a new twenty-thousand-square-foot Visitors' and Exhibit Center with flexible exhibition, interpretive and classroom space in celebration of its fortieth anniversary. This event reflects the continued efforts of the Baton Rouge community to assure the future of the LSU Rural Life Museum and Windrush Gardens. After the development of a business plan for expansion, the Whispers of Change campaign was launched by the board of trustees, the Friends of the LSU Rural Life Museum, the museum staff and the community. The campaign's purpose was to fund five objectives: alleviate physical and environmental threats to the collections; bring existing facilities into compliance with safety and accessibility codes; enhance the visitor experience through improved facilities; increase revenue; and expand educational programs.

The LSU Rural Life Museum and Windrush Gardens' success, even before the campaign, was clear as shown by the growth of the number of visitors from the invitation of a very select few for the first open house in 1971 to more than sixty thousand visitors from throughout the city, state and world in 2008. Volunteers and staff, and the educational outreach programs they have established, are the reason why the number of visitors grows each year.

Daily activities for visitors at the Rural Life Museum and Windrush Gardens include permanent and rotating exhibitions of the artifacts collection; tours, self-guided or docent led; and special programs. Artifacts in the museum's collection are used in the buildings on the grounds to aid in interpretation of

Groundbreaking for the Visitors' and Exhibit Center was done by mule and plow rather than by traditional shovels. *Courtesy of Jim Zietz, LSU University Relations.*

The wooden wall behind the statue moves to open the meeting room in the Visitors' and Exhibit Center. *Courtesy of the LSU Rural Life Museum and Windrush Gardens.*

Above: The large Visitors' and Exhibit Center can accommodate artifacts as big as a wagon. *Courtesy of the LSU Rural Life Museum and Windrush Gardens.*

Right: Students from grades six through twelve serve in the junior docent program. *Courtesy of Darelyn Marshall, the LSU Rural Life Museum and Windrush Gardens.*

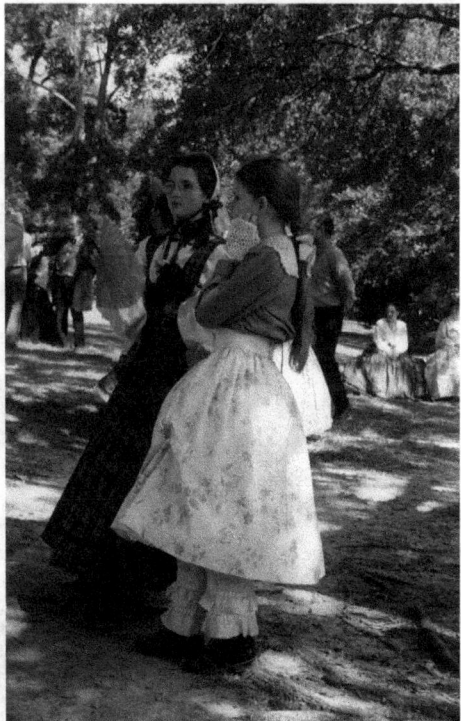

everyday rural life in Louisiana. The artifacts date from prehistoric times to the early twentieth century. The majority of the collections exhibited in the barn are arranged to reflect and interpret the lives of Native Americans in Louisiana; slavery; industrial development; military conflicts; farming and other livelihoods such as hunting and trapping; and other related topics.

Docents, volunteers who lead tours and discussions at the museum and gardens, have been critical to the success of the programs since the early 1990s. Through an effective and extensive training program, more than one hundred volunteer docents are prepared to conduct guided tours for school groups of all ages, adult groups and international tours, sometimes in the visitors' native language. Many visitors who are not part of organized tours or school groups interact with the docents as well. The background

Many artisans demonstrate nineteenth-century activities such as woodcarving that were part of daily life in rural Louisiana. *Courtesy of the LSU Rural Life Museum and Windrush Gardens.*

Groups performing folk and traditional music are always crowd pleasers at annual events.
Courtesy of the LSU Rural Life Museum and Windrush Gardens.

of the docents is varied, and their knowledge and experience add to their interpretive skills. A program for junior docents was added, and fifty-five volunteers from grades six through twelve assist with educational programs and events. The junior docents are asked to attend mandatory meetings and training sessions and commit to donating thirty hours of time during a year. They are taught by senior docents and the museum staff. A Rural Life Apprentice Program has been established for children from the fourth through the eighth grades. During the program, students are taught by artisans and docents.[122]

Each year, the LSU Rural Life Museum and Windrush Gardens presents several annual events designed to extend its educational activities and community outreach. Most events at the Rural Life Museum feature artisans of crafts and skills of rural Louisianans in the nineteenth century such as blacksmithing, bonnet making, candle making, chair weaving, cloth dying, pottery making and woodworking. In October, during Harvest Days, visitors are invited to experience corn grinding, open-hearth cooking, syrup making and woodcutting and woodcarving through living history demonstrations

Staff members and artisans reflect on their activities. *Courtesy of Darelyn Marshall, the LSU Rural Life Museum and Windrush Gardens.*

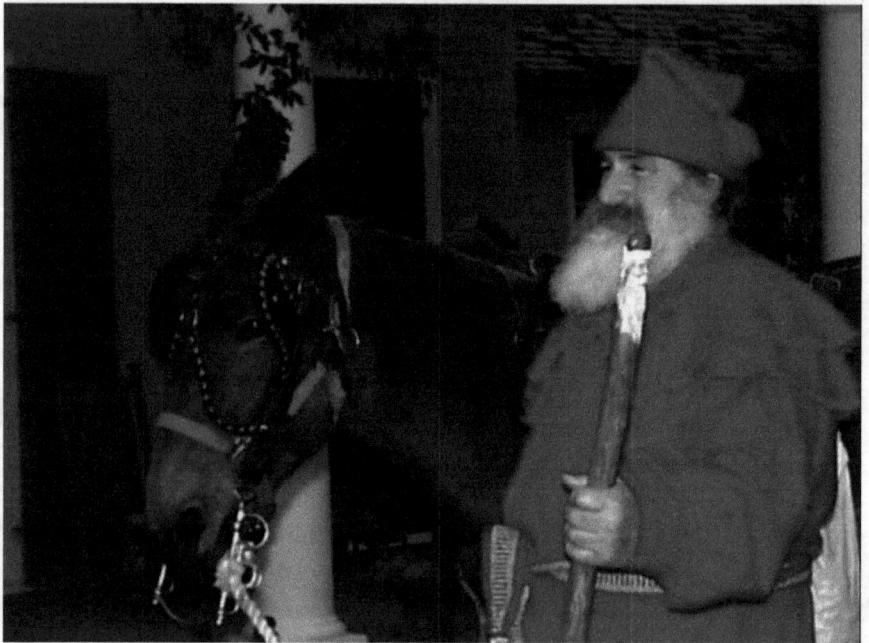

Papa Noel arriving at the Rural Life Christmas. *Courtesy of the LSU Rural Life Museum and Windrush Gardens.*

and to learn how these activities were necessary to rural life. A Rural Life Christmas each December interprets for visitors Louisiana country holiday activities including artisan demonstrations, folk music, folk decorations, a visit by Papa Noel (instead of Santa Claus) and a traditional Louisiana bonfire to light the way for Papa Noel. At both events, Civil War reenactors and storytellers have appeared.

One of the oldest events is the Ione E. Burden Symposium held each spring, which focuses on, and presents current research about, the topics and periods represented in the museum's collections and the gardens' specimens and history. Expert speakers from many fields of study and work share their perspectives on rural life and gardening in the eighteenth, nineteenth and early twentieth centuries.

Other opportunities for the public appreciation of Louisiana rural life include the Old Fashioned Easter Celebration held since 2008, as well as several events that began during the fortieth anniversary year including an annual soirée; Haints, Haunts and Halloween: A Rural Fall Fair; and a May open house with free admission. Most activities serve the purpose of education but are also part of fundraising events for the LSU Rural Life Museum and Windrush Gardens. Also, since 2005, the Zapp's International Beerfest has been a popular community and fundraising event.

The twenty-fifth anniversary of the museum was celebrated in 1995, and the official name changed to the LSU Rural Life Museum and Windrush Gardens. In 1997, staff and docents formed Friends of the LSU Rural Life Museum to benefit the museum and gardens through publicity, outreach and fundraising, focused on continuing the work of Steele Burden, who died in 1995. Since 1998, the Friends have sponsored Evening at Windrush as a way to celebrate the history of Windrush Plantation through a traditional nineteenth-century southern dinner at the Windrush House, with after-dinner strolls through the gardens. Friends of the LSU Rural Life Museum was instrumental in the success of the Whispers of Change campaign to build the new Visitors' and Exhibit Center that opened in 2010.

Another aid to the continued growth and development of the museum and gardens was the establishment in 2000 of the LSU Board of Trustees for the Rural Life Museum, members of which also served as leaders for the campaign and who will oversee planning for future growth. The board's purpose is to advise the officials of LSU and the Burden Foundation on strategic plans, development and promotion. Representatives from LSU, the LSU AgCenter, the Burden Foundation and the public constitute the members of the board of trustees.[123]

Over a five-year period, more than $5 million in gifts was received to complete the Whispers of Change campaign. Honorary chairs John Barton Sr., Dr. Paul Murrill and Sue Turner, as well as and general chairs John and Frances Monroe, led generous community support for the campaign. Imo Brown provided the first $1 million to the campaign before her death in 2008. Friends of the Rural Life Museum raised $500,000. The Burden Foundation gave $1 million. The new addition was designed by Architects Southwest of Lafayette. "Always mindful that the Burden family's vision for the museum and adjacent Windrush Gardens was to preserve the rural setting and feel of 'days gone by,' great care was taken in developing these plans."[124]

The Burden Foundation was also critical to the success of the campaign. Created in 1961 by Pike, Ione and Steele for the purpose of administering their donations of Windrush Plantation land to LSU, the foundation's board has grown from four to eighteen members representing the Burden family and the community. For forty years, the Burden Foundation has made significant gifts to the Rural Life Museum and Windrush Gardens in

Paintings and sculptures collected by Steele are displayed throughout the Visitors' and Exhibit Center. *Courtesy of the LSU Rural Life Museum and Windrush Gardens.*

addition to the 440 acres. The Burden Foundation has from its beginning acted as an advisory group to all units of the Burden Center, including the museum. It encourages development and utilization of the entire Burden Center through financial donations used for special projects and events, day-to-day operations and planning.[125]

As part of the Whispers of Change campaign the museum completed a revised master plan in 2006 that included the development of sixteen new acres of land. The campaign accomplished five components necessary to ensure the Rural Life Museum's continued growth and success: alleviated the physical threat to museum collections by adding systems for fire suppression, security and air conditioning; brought existing facilities into electrical, plumbing and accessibility compliance; enhanced future visitors' experiences through updated facilities, new gallery space and a new visitors'

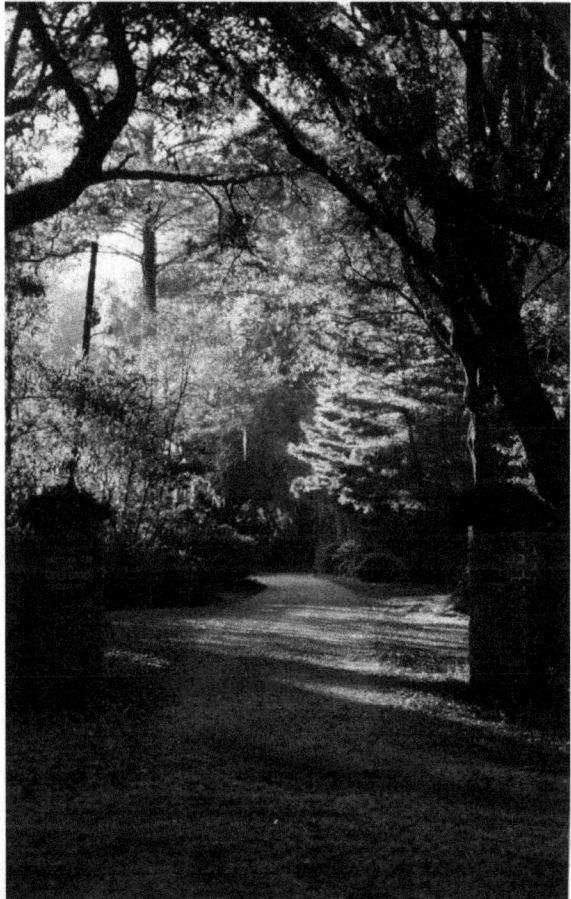

Everyone at the Rural Life Museum hopes that you will visit often. *Courtesy of Darelyn Marshall, the LSU Rural Life Museum and Windrush Gardens.*

center; and expanded the educational programs through the development of new and broader programs for schoolchildren, college students and the general public. The original exhibit barn was incorporated into the new Visitors' and Exhibit Center and connected by a wall of glass. The barn is itself an artifact, as its walls were Steele Burden's canvas on which he wrote, drew and painted his thoughts and images of Louisiana life. His artistic impressions set the overall theme of the Rural Life Museum exhibits.[126]

With the completion and opening of the Visitors' and Exhibit Center in 2010, the LSU Rural Life Museum embarked on a permanent exhibition plan based on commemoration, preservation and education that is rooted in the museum's mission to increase the appreciation of Louisiana's heritage and way of life by preserving the architecture and artifacts from nineteenth-century rural Louisiana. Within the seven thousand feet of exhibition space, seven areas serve as an introduction to the outdoor collections of exhibits, vernacular architecture and special collections that focus on the interpretation of the life of rural, working-class Louisianans from the eighteenth through the early twentieth century.

When Emma Gertrude Barbee Burden and her husband, John Charles Burden, first saw their new home in 1856, it was over five hundred acres of woodlands with only a few acres cleared for crops and raising cattle. Perhaps they accepted the permission to live there from her uncle, William Stephen Pike, with some trepidation about their future as farmers. Still, they embraced the land, made it their home and named it Windrush Plantation. Emma and John left Windrush as a legacy to their family and to the people of Baton Rouge, Louisiana, who have embraced it as well.

NOTES

INTRODUCTION

1. The Ione Burden Family Papers, Louisiana and Lower Mississippi Valley Collections, Louisiana State University Libraries, Inventory. Hereafter cited as Burden Family Papers, LLMVC, LSU Libraries.
2. Rural Life Museum, *The LSU Rural Life Museum* (Baton Rouge, LA: LSU Public Relations, n.d.), 2.
3. LSU Rural Life Museum and Windrush Gardens website, http://appl027.lsu.edu/rlm/rurallifeweb.nsf/index.
4. Ibid.
5. Burden Family Papers, LLMVC, LSU Libraries; Rural Life Museum website; Rural Life Museum scrapbooks.
6. Burden Family Papers, LLMVC, LSU Libraries.
7. Ibid., "Act of Donation" draft, 1964.
8. *Baton Rouge Advocate*, January 8, 2010.

CHAPTER 1

9. Sylvia Frank Rodrigue and Faye Phillips, *Historic Baton Rouge: An Illustrated History* (San Antonio, TX: Historical Publishing Network, 2006), 13–16.
10. John Monroe, "The Origins of Windrush," Burden Horticulture Society *Reflections and Visions* 2 (April 2009): 1; Marie Adrien Persac, *Plantations on*

the Mississippi River from Natchez to New Orleans, 1858 (Gretna, LA: Pelican Publishing Company, 1967).

11. "The Bank of Baton Rouge Built by Public Confidence," *State Times Morning Advocate*, July 2, 1919; Burden Family Papers, LLMVC, LSU Libraries; Alcée Fortier, ed., *Louisiana*, vol. 3 (Chicago, IL: Century Historical Association, 1914), 244–46.

12. Family information is taken from Louisiana census records via Ancestory. com and John Monroe, "Origins of Windrush," Burden Horticulture Society *Reflections and Visions* 2 (April 2009): 1; John Monroe, "The Descendants of John Charles and Emma Gertrude Burden," Burden Horticulture Society *Reflections and Visions* 2 (August 2009): 1; John Monroe, "The Burdens Return to Windrush," Burden Horticulture Society *Reflections and Visions* 2 (October 2009): 1; John Monroe, "The Women of Windrush," Burden Horticulture Society *Reflections and Visions* 2 (December 2009): 1; Burden Family Papers, LLMVC, LSU Libraries; Rodrigue and Phillips, *Historic Baton Rouge*, 17–21.

13. Correspondence, April 30, 1880, Burden Family Papers, LLMVC, LSU Libraries; Fortier, *Louisiana*, 415–16.

14. *Biographical and Historical Memoires of Louisiana*, vol. 2 (Chicago, IL: Goodspeed Publishing Company, 1892), 405–7.

15. "Mercantile Bank Absorbs Capital City Bank," *State Times*, December 7, 1916; Fortier, *Louisiana*, 415–16; Annabelle Armstrong, "'Miss Ollie' presides graciously over 'Windrush' where tradition abounds: 83-year old Mrs. William Pike Burden, Sr. cares for garden, cattle too, and keeps informed on everything," *State Times*, January 19, 1955; Burden Family Papers, LLMVC, LSU Libraries.

16. Steele Burden oral history interview with Kathy Grigsby, Mss. 4700.0452, LLMVC, LSU Libraries, 1994.

17. Business card of W.P. Burden, candidate for commissioner public parks and streets, undated, Burden Family Papers, LLMVC, LSU Libraries.

18. Steele-Williams wedding invitation, October 10, 1906, and Tom Jenkins to Pike Burden, March 24, 1919, and Williams obituary, March 16, 1951, and Ione to Peggy Tuesch, 1951, Burden Family Papers, LLMVC, LSU Libraries.

19. O.B. Steele Jr. obituary, *State Times*, May 17, 1949, Burden Family Papers, LLMVC, LSU Libraries.

20. Armstrong, "Miss Ollie," *State Times*, January 19, 1955.

21. Ibid.; Burden interview with Grigsby, 1994.

22. Armstrong, "Miss Ollie," *State Times*, January 19, 1955.

23. Ibid.

24. Ibid.; C.A. Yancy, Stables drawing, January 19, 1911, Burden Family Papers, LLMVC, LSU Libraries; Burden interview with Grigsby, 1994.

25. Armstrong, "Miss Ollie," *State Times*, January 19, 1955.

26. Ibid.

27. J.S. Herget to Dr. John Melton, pastor, First Presbyterian Church, July 3, 1958, Burden Family Papers, LLMVC, LSU Libraries.

28. Ibid.

29. Box 2, Folder 11, Burden Family Papers, LLMVC, LSU Libraries.

30. *Times Picayune*, August 11, 1946; circa 1946–47 memoir, unsigned, Burden Family Papers, LLMVC, LSU Libraries.

31. *State Times*, January 16, 1957; "Pike Burden Airport" at Windrush Plantation, license, June 19, 1937, Louisiana Department of Public Works' Aeronautics Division, Burden Family Papers, LLMVC, LSU Libraries.

32. *Morning Advocate*, October 30, 1960.

33. Burden Family Papers, LLMVC, LSU Libraries.

34. *State Times*, April 1951, May 1952 and August 25, 1995.

35. *Morning Advocate*, June 6, 1972.

36. Ione to Dr. Chandler, president, College of William and Mary, December 8, 1932, and Ruth Heidelberg, secretary to the president, LSU, to Ione, December 28, 1932, Burden Family Papers, LLMVC, LSU Libraries; Burden interview with Grigsby, 1994.

37. Power to Frey, April 24, 1947, and Ione Burden to Power and Cole, April 25, 1947, Burden Family Papers, LLMVC, LSU Libraries.

38. *Morning Advocate*, December 1938, September 19, 1948; *State Times*, September 25, 1946.

39. LSU president to Ione, August 17, 1950, LSU; "Dedicatory Program for the LSU Centennial Celebration," April 1960, Burden Family Papers, LLMVC, LSU Libraries.

40. Ibid.

41. Helen Gordon to Ione, June 30, 1966, Burden Family Papers, LLMVC, LSU Libraries.

42. Steele to Ione, August, 1950, Burden Family Papers, LLMVC, LSU Libraries.

43. Ione to Mama, June 19, 1931, and Ione to Mr. and Mrs. Harold Stokes, February 18, 1960, Burden Family Papers, LLMVC, LSU Libraries.

44. Ione to Mama, March 7, 1929, Burden Family Papers, LLMVC, LSU Libraries.

45. Ione to Deanie, February 28, 1929, Burden Family Papers, LLMVC, LSU Libraries.

46. Ione to Mama, April, May 1929, Burden Family Papers, LLMVC, LSU Libraries.

47. Ione to T. Boyd, March 31, 1932, Burden Family Papers, LLMVC, LSU Libraries.

48. Ione to William Schatz, April 17, 1959, and Mrs. Ernest A. Gueymard to Ione, April 29, 1967, and Ione to Paul W. Murrill, April 1, 1975, and Foundation for Historical Louisiana to Ione, August 6, 1975, Burden Family Papers, LLMVC, LSU Libraries.

49. Drafts of "Act of Donation," 1964, Burden Family Papers, LLMVC, LSU Libraries.

50. Alvin Rubin to Ione Burden, August 23, 1966, and Alvin Rubin to Frank W. Middleton of Taylor, Porter, Brooks and Phillips, October 1966, and Burden Foundation Board of Directors Minutes, May 10, 1967, and May 12, 1970, Burden Family Papers, LLMVC, LSU Libraries; Jeff Kuehny, "One of a Kind Gift," *Reflections and Visions* 2 (2009): 3.

51. Alvin Rubin to R. Paul Greene, August 6, 1963, Burden Family Papers, LLMVC, LSU Libraries; *Morning Advocate*, September 9, 1964.

52. Rubin to Pike, Ione and Steele, August 24, 1963, and Rubin to R. Paul Greene, September 17, 1963, and Rubin to Burdens, November 18, 1963, and Sister Gertrude to Ione and Steele, March 28 and December 21, 1966, Burden Family Papers, LLMVC, LSU Libraries; *Morning Advocate*, September 5 and 15, 1964.

53. Burden Family Papers, Inventory, LLMVC, LSU Libraries; *Morning Advocate*, June 19, 1974, and August 26, 1979.

54. *Sunday Advocate/State Times* magazine, November 16, 1980, and February 7, 1982; *Sunday Advocate*, July 29, 1984; Steele Burden oral history interview with Suzanne Turner, Mss. 4700.0318, LLMVC, LSU Libraries, 1993.

CHAPTER 2

55. *Sunday Advocate*, July 29, 1984; Bob Anderson, "Inside Report: This Yard Man Has Left his Mark on Baton Rouge," *Advocate*, July 13, 1994.

56. *Sunday Advocate*, July 29, 1984.

57. Peggy Cox, "Steele Burden and His Masterpiece: Windrush Gardens," *State-by-State Gardening* (2005): 12–16; Burden interview with Turner, 1993; *Sunday Advocate*, July 29, 1984.

58. Steele Burden interview with Grigsby, 1994; Cox, "Steele Burden," 12–16; Sarah Sue Goldsmith, "Windrush Gardens Offer Up Nature's Beauty," *Sunday Advocate* (April 30, 1995); Burden interview with Turner, 1993.

59. Cox, "Steele Burden," 12–16; Burden interview with Turner, 1993; *Sunday Advocate,* July 29, 1984.

60. Cox, "Steele Burden," 14–15.

61. Ibid.; Goldsmith, "Windrush Gardens."

62. Ibid.; Burden interview with Turner, 1993.

63. Burden interview with Turner, 1993.

64. Cox, "Steele Burden," 16.

65. Goldsmith, "Windrush Gardens."

66. *Times Picayune*, October 27, 1919, and November 27, 1921; Burden interview with Turner, 1993; Cox, "Steele Burden," 14.

67. *Times Picayune*, October 27, 1919, and November 27, 1921.

68. Cox, "Steele Burden," 14; Ione to Miss Ollie and Steele, February 20, 1931, Burden Family Papers, LLMVC, LSU Libraries; Burden interview with Turner, 1993; Anderson, "Inside Report"; *Sunday Advocate,* July 29, 1984.

69. Burden interview with Turner, 1993.

70. Ibid.; Burden interview with Grigsby, 1994.

71. Burden interview with Turner, 1993; Burden interview with Grigsby, 1994.

72. Ibid.

73. Ibid.

74. Dudley Fricke oral history interview with Douglas Davis, Mss. 4700.0813, LLMVC, LSU Libraries, 1997.

75. Fricke interview with Davis, 1997.

76. *Baton Rouge Enterprise*, July 9–15, 1981; *Sunday Advocate*, July 29, 1984; Burden interview with Turner, 1993.

77. Ibid.; Burden interview with Turner, 1993.

78. Sally T. Kuzenski, "A Day in the Life: John E. Dutton, Registrar and Conservator, Rural Life Museum," *LSU Today* 6 (August 27, 1989): 1.

79. Mary Ann Sternberg, *Along the River Road: Past and Present on Louisiana's Historic Byway* (Baton Rouge, LA: LSU Press, 1996), 142–44.

80. Burden interview with Turner, 1993.

81. Anderson, "Inside Report"; *Sunday Advocate,* July 29, 1984.

82. Burden interview with Grigsby, 1994; Burden interview with Turner, 1993.

83. Burden interview with Grigsby, 1994; Burden interview with Turner, 1993; *Advocate*, February 5, 1995.

84. Sternberg, *Along the River Road*, 184; Burden interview with Turner, 1993; *Times Picayune*, August 18, 1938.

85. Burden Family Papers, Inventory, LLMVC, LSU Libraries; *Sunday Advocate*, July 29, 1984.

86. Burden interview with Turner, 1993.

87. Anderson, "Inside Report."

88. Ibid.; Burden interview with Turner, 1993.

89. Steele to Ione, August, 1950, Burden Family Papers, LLMVC, LSU Libraries.

90. Anderson, "Inside Report"; Burden interview with Grigsby, 1994.

91. Burden interview with Grigsby, 1994.

92. Burden interview with Turner, 1993.

93. Ibid.; *Sunday Advocate*, July 29, 1984; Burden interview with Grigsby, 1994.

94. Trees & Trails website, www.treesandtrails.com; *Advocate*, November 10, 2009; Merikaye Presley, "LSU's Eloquent Relic of Ante-bellum Days," *Dixie* magazine (November 12, 1972): 63.

95. *LSU AgCenter Newsletter*, "Burden Center: Baton Rouge Jewel Dedicated to Horticulture Research," April 16, 2009, www.lsuagcenter.com; Sara Sue Goldsmith, "LSU's Orangerie Will Open to Public June 18," LSU News Service news release, LSU University Relations, June 9, 1998.

96. *Advocate*, March 15, 1995.

Chapter 3

97. *Daily Reveille*, August 31, 1972; Presley, "LSU's Eloquent Relic," 60; *Advocate*, January 8, 2010.

98. *Sunday Advocate*, April 23, 1967; *Advocate*, January 8, 2010.

99. Sternberg, *Along the River Road*, 72–73, 76–78.

100. Ibid., 63, 66.

101. Ibid., 78; Richard Follett, *The Sugar Masters: Planters and Slaves in Louisiana's Cane World, 1820–1860* (Baton Rouge, LA: LSU Press, 2005), 11–12; Bennett H. Wall, ed., *Louisiana: A History*, 4th ed. (Wheeling, IL: Harlan Davidson, 2002), 134–35.

102. Ibid.

103. Sternberg, *Along the River Road*, 69; Wall, *Louisiana*, 134–35; Rural Life Museum (hereafter RLM), *The LSU Rural Life Museum*, 17; J. Frazer Smith, *Plantation Houses and Mansions of the Old South* (New York: Dover, 1993), 197; descriptions of vernacular buildings throughout this chapter are from the

Rural Life Museum *Docents' Manual*, 1998, 2005, which has unnumbered pages, and those descriptions are not footnoted individually.

104. Wall, *Louisiana*, 134–35; Follett, *Sugar Masters*, 12–13.

105. Follett, *Sugar Masters*, 125.

106. RLM, *The LSU Rural Life Museum*, 11.

107. Wall, *Louisiana*, 159, 161.

108. RLM, *The LSU Rural Life Museum*, 14–15; *State Times*, April 4, 1975.

109. RLM, *The LSU Rural Life Museum*, 10.

110. Ibid., 16; *Dixie* magazine (November 12, 1972).

111. Wall, *Louisiana*, 170; RLM, *The LSU Rural Life Museum*, 19; Rural Life Museum website.

112. Wall, *Louisiana*, 193–94; RLM, *The LSU Rural Life Museum*, 20.

113. Gaines Glass, "Fragment of a Refrain," *Register* (July 1979); Claire Olsen, "Controversial Statue Could Be Moved," October 5, 2009, www.wafb.com.

114. RLM, *The LSU Rural Life Museum*, 21.

115. Ibid.

116. Ibid.; Wall, *Louisiana*, 139, 170.

117. RLM, *The LSU Rural Life Museum*, 21.

118. Ibid.; Wall, *Louisiana*, 139.

119. *Baton Rouge Enterprise*, September 27–October 3, 1979.

120. Sternberg, *Along the River Road*, 96.

121. Wall, *Louisiana*, 71.

Chapter 4

122. Chris Russo Blackwood, "Old-fashioned Holiday: Steel Burden's Spirit Lives on at Rural Life Museum," *InRegister* (December 2009): 28.

123. David Floyd, "LSU Rural Life Museum Business Plan for Museum Expansion" (Baton Rouge, LA: LSU Rural Life Museum, 2006), 3.

124. *LSU Today*, January 15, 2010; *Advocate*, January 22, 2010; Rural Life Museum, *Whispers of Change Campaign* (Baton Rouge, LA: LSU Rural Life Museum, 2008), 3–5.

125. Tonja Normand, "Corporate Partner Profile," *Whispers of the Past* 16 (Winter 2009): 5.

126. Rural Life Museum website; Carol Anne Biltzer, "Old Meets New," *Advocate*, January 8, 2010.

INDEX

ABOUT THE AUTHOR

Faye Phillips is associate dean of LSU Libraries at Louisiana State University in Baton Rouge. She has worked in various positions at the LSU Libraries since 1986. Phillips has published books and articles on local and Louisiana history and library topics. She earned bachelor's and master's degrees in American history from Georgia State University in Atlanta and a master's degree in library science from the University of North Carolina at Chapel Hill.

www.ingramcontent.com/pod-product-compliance
Lightning Source LLC
Chambersburg PA
CBHW071941260326
41914CB00004B/713